Shrubs & Hedges

Created and designed by
the editorial staff of
ORTHO BOOKS

Editor
Cedric Crocker

Writers
A. Cort Sinnes
Michael McKinley

Illustrator
Ron Hildebrand

Designer
Gary Hespenheide

Ortho Books

Publisher
Edward A. Evans

Editorial Director
Christine Jordan

Production Director
Ernie S. Tasaki

Managing Editors
Michael D. Smith
Sally W. Smith

System Manager
Linda M. Bouchard

National Sales Manager
J. D. Gillis

**National Accounts Manager—
Book Trade**
Paul D. Wiedemann

Marketing Specialist
Dennis M. Castle

Distribution Specialist
Barbara F. Steadham

Operations Assistant
Georgiann Wright

Administrative Assistant
Francine Lorentz-Olson

Technical Consultant
J. A. Crozier, Jr., Ph.D.

Address all inquiries to:
Ortho Books
Box 5006
San Ramon, CA 94583-0906

Copyright © 1980, 1990
Monsanto Company
All rights reserved under international and
Pan-American copyright conventions.

8	9	10	11	12	13
95	96	97	98	99	00

ISBN 0-89721-223-1
Library of Congress Catalog Card
Number 90-80074

THE SOLARIS GROUP
2527 Camino Ramon
San Ramon, CA 94583

Acknowledgments

Consultants
Fred Galle, Curator, Callaway Gardens,
   Pine Mountain, GA
Jane Gates, Helen Crocker Library, Strybing
   Arboretum, San Francisco, Calif.
Richard Hildreth, Director, State Arboretum
   of Utah, Salt Lake City, Utah
Dr. Joseph E. Howland, Professor of
   Horticulture, University of Nevada
Paul W. Meyer, Curator, Morris Arboretum,
   Chestnut Hill, Penn.
Jonathan T. Plant, Jonathan Plant Associates,
   Lafayette, Calif.

Photo Editor
Sarah Bendersky

Copy Chief
Melinda E. Levine

Editorial Coordinator
Cass Dempsey

Copyeditor
Andrew Alden

Proofreader
Deborah Bruner

Indexer
Trisha Feuerstein

Editorial Assistants
John Parr
Laurie A. Steele

Composition by
Nancy P. McCune

Layout and production by
Lezlly Freier

Separations by
Color Tech Corporation

Lithographed in the USA by
Banta Company

Special Thanks to
Louisa Arbuckle, Menlo Park, Calif.
Burlingame Garden Center, Burlingame, Calif.
Menlo Park Library, Menlo Park, Calif.
Orchard Nursery, Lafayette, Calif.
Jane Wilson

Photographers
Names of photographers are followed by the page numbers
on which their work appears. R = right, C = center, L = left,
T = top, B = bottom.

William C. Aplin: 62R

Liz Ball: 8T, 13B, 77R, 80R, 81L, 92, 99

Laurie A. Black: 13T, 67R, 76L

Josephine Coatsworth: 7

Michael A. Dirr: 32, 42T, 54T, 54B, 59BR, 64L, 64R, 70L,
   71BL, 74L, 76R, 78L, 80L, 84R, 91BL, 96L, 97L, 103L, 106R,
   107L

Thomas E. Eltzroth: 59L, 68R, 71TL, 72R, 73L, 75R, 79L, 89R,
   90TL, 90R, 91TL, 95BR, 96R

Derek Fell: 65TR, 66L, 67L, 69L, 79BR, 83R, 93R, 94TR,
   95TR, 104R 105TR

Saxon Holt: 1, 4, 9B, 10T, 10C, 11, 12C, 12B, 39T, 53, 55,
   59TR, 61

Sandra Ivany: 10B, 44B

Michael Landis: 57TL, 60R, 91R

Robert E. Lyons: 57TR, 65L, 68L, 69TR, 70R, 71TR, 71BR,
   77TL, 77BL, 88R, back cover BL

Michael McKinley: Front cover, 6, 14T, 14B, 16, 19, 20T,
   22BL, 22BR, 23TR, 24, 34, 36, 39B, 42B, 46B, 48, 49T, 50, 56,
   57BL, 58, 65BR, 69BR, 83L, 84L, 87TL, 87BL, 94L, 102R,
   104L, 105L, 105BR, 107R, back cover TL

Tovah Martin: 74R, 78R, 94BR

Jack Napton: 66BR, 87R

Ortho Information Services: 20B, 89L, 103R, back cover TR,
   back cover BR

Photo/Nats, David M. Stone: 62L; Ann Reilly: 72L

Martin Schweitzer: 25T, 40

John J. Smith: 60L, 66TR, 73R, 75L, 79TR, 81R, 85L, 86L,
   86R, 88L, 90BL, 93L, 95L, 97L, 98, 100R, 101L, 101R, 102L,
   105BR

Michael D. Smith: 46T, 47

Connie Toops: 82L, 82R, 85R, 100L

Tom Tracy: 8B

Valan Photos, A. B. Joyce: 12T

Wolf von dem Bussche: 9T

Front Cover
Shrubs and hedges line the path to a garden retreat.

Back Cover
Top left: Well-trimmed evergreen hedges form the
backbone of the formal garden style.

Top right: Shrubs provide a rich variety of year-round
color. This red-leafed burning-bush (*Euonymus alata*)
presents a striking winter contrast to the deciduous and
evergreen trees behind it.

Bottom left: Shrubs can be trained and shaped to meet
many needs, as with this firethorn (*Pyracantha coccinea*),
grown to add color and interest to a bare city wall.

Bottom right: Flowering shrubs—such as these
rhododendrons and azaleas—are available in a wide variety
of blossom colors and shapes.

Title Page
The variety available in shrubs and hedges is apparent in
this garden setting—arching boughs of beautybush
(*Kolkwitzia amabilis*) shade the stone bench and boxwood
(*Buxus sempervirens*) lines the path.

DESIGNING WITH SHRUBS AND HEDGES

Shrubs and hedges are the workhorses of garden design. They can provide color and beauty, traffic control, security, private places, or protection from wind and sun.

PLANNING, BUYING, AND PLANTING

Careful planning before buying and planting shrubs will help you make the best choices. Select healthy plants and follow proper planting techniques.

THE BASICS OF CARE

Shrubs are among the easiest of plants to care for. The right fertilizer at the right time, effective watering, protection from adverse weather, and solving common problems as they arise will help shrubs thrive.

PRUNING

Pruning is essential to the maintenance of most garden shrubs. It is also a way to shape shrubs to meet the design needs of the garden. Proper pruning requires knowing some basic pruning techniques.

PLANT SELECTION GUIDE

One of the most valuable tools for any gardener is a good plant list. This chapter includes lists of shrubs for specific uses followed by complete descriptions of each.

Shrubs & Hedges

Designing With Shrubs and Hedges

Shrubs and hedges are the workhorses of garden design. They can provide color and beauty, traffic control, security, private places, or protection from wind and sun.

Shrubs offer the gardener many beautiful and dramatic possibilities. There are thousands of varieties of shrubs in every form and size imaginable—an array of shapes, textures, and year-round colors that seems almost infinite. But because shrubs are so familiar, sometimes their special traits are overlooked.

Shrubs are a key unifying element in the garden. They reinforce horticultural groupings or themes of the basic design, and used in masses, they can define spaces and guide the eye. Shrubs can create privacy, accentuate doorways and entrances, and hide unsightly views. They can improve the climate of the yard and even help to protect against burglary. And they can accomplish these purposes with a minimum of maintenance. They can also serve as garden highlights.

Hedges have been a part of gardening for as long as there have been gardens. In spite of their upkeep demands, they not only are considered an integral part of many gardens, but also provide many ways to define and protect areas of the garden. Virtually any shrub can be trained or shaped to serve as a hedge.

This book contains the necessary information for a wide range of gardening situations, from landscaping an entire yard, to looking for a single shrub for a special place, to caring for existing shrubs. How to design with, buy, plant, transplant, water, fertilize, and prune are covered in the chapters that follow. The "Plant Selection Guide" (see page 51) provides detailed information on specific shrubs to help you make the best selections for your garden.

The range of evergreen and deciduous shrubs, with blooms of every color, offers almost endless possibilities for garden design.

WHAT IS A SHRUB?

Although there is no one definition for shrubs, they are usually described as woody plants—with multiple stems or trunks—that grow to less than 15 feet high when mature.

A woody plant is one with stems and branches that survive from one year to the next and that do not die back to the ground after each growing season. Their woody nature distinguishes shrubs from herbaceous plants, which are subject to winter damage and die back to the ground each year.

The fact that shrubs have multiple stems or trunks sets them apart from trees, which usually have a single trunk. Shrubs trained to a single trunk are called standards and are often used for a formal effect.

Although the same plants reach widely varying mature heights in different regions, shrubs generally grow to less than 15 feet, and trees exceed that height. But a shrub that grows taller than 15 feet isn't necessarily regarded as a tree. Most trees are capable of reaching impressive heights, but shrubs remain comparatively small—somewhere in the vicinity of 15 feet.

WHAT IS A HEDGE?

Hedges are formed from shrubs that are planted close together to form an unbroken line and, in most cases, are carefully trimmed. Formal hedges are similar to fences in their solid, even appearance. A hedge is a way of delineating space, forming a garden border or property boundary, or creating a screen for privacy. Just about any shrub can be used to make a hedge, but some shrubs lend themselves more than others to regular trimming and uniform growth. A list of shrubs that are particularly good for hedges begins on page 62.

Hedge shrubs come in three basic heights: low—12 inches or less—for bordering flower beds and walks; medium—up to 6 feet—used for property boundaries and as backdrops for other plants; and tall—over 6 feet—for controlling wind and sun and screening out undesirable views.

Specific information about planting, trimming, and maintaining hedges is included in the following chapters. In all other respects, shrubs commonly used as hedge plantings are treated in this book like other shrubs.

This trimmed hedge creates a transition between massed shrubs and a lawn.

DECIDUOUS AND EVERGREEN SHRUBS

Shrubs may be deciduous or evergreen. Deciduous plants lose their leaves in the fall and grow new leaves in the spring. Deciduous shrubs known for their spring flowers, such as lilacs, need sufficient winter chilling to put on their best spring display. These shrubs can be grown in mild-winter areas, but their flowering is more limited.

Evergreen plants keep their leaves the year around and are divided into two major categories: broad-leafed evergreens and coniferous (cone-bearing) evergreens. Generally speaking, the broad-leafed evergreens tend to be more tender than deciduous shrubs, and they find their widest adaptability in areas with mild winters. Coniferous evergreens grow in most climates and may be found in almost every part of the United States.

The surest way to grow shrubs successfully is to choose varieties that you know are hardy for your climate—refer to the "Plant Selection Guide" on page 51.

FORMS OF SHRUBS

To pick the right shrub for each garden area, it's important to know the form of the plant when mature. Often a shrub changes considerably from purchase in a 5-gallon can to maturity after several years in the garden. Most shrubs develop into their own naturally occurring form. A shrub does best if allowed to develop in its own way rather than trying to make it into something it is not.

Influences on Form

The form a shrub takes depends on its species and on the way it is pruned, as well as on its location in the garden. For a shrub to be dense and full, plant it in full sun. For one that has a lacy, open look, plant the shrub in diffused sunlight. The extent to which light levels affect the shape of a shrub depends on the shrub. Some shrubs have the same shape no matter what light level they receive; others look like two different species in sun and shade. For example, Japanese maples are open, spreading, and graceful when grown in a shady location but compact and globular when grown in the sun.

In nature, shrubs form much of the understory of forests—the plants that grow beneath

the tree canopy. These understory plants spread their branches to catch the little light that penetrates the trees above. Their leaves are arranged in horizontal planes, with no leaf under another; thus, understory shrubs have an open, delicate, and graceful habit.

Shrubs that grow in full sun, in meadows or brushland, grow smaller and are more closely knit. Because there is no shortage of light, their problem is one of exposure to sun, wind, rain, and snow. A compact form, with small leaves packed tightly together and stems that are short and thick, gives shrubs protection from the elements.

Shrubs grown in containers can be used to add color and interest to a garden patio. Fuchsias are available in a multitude of varieties and are an ideal container plant.

Top: The design of this garden is almost entirely composed of the trimmed and natural shapes of shrubs and hedges. Bottom: Shrubs with spreading shapes— such as this juniper— are well suited for ground covers.

Natural Forms of Shrubs

Shrubs are usually divided into eight categories according to their natural form.

These basic forms are indicated in the shrub descriptions in the "Plant Selection Guide" (see page 51).

Pyramidal   With their neat shape, common to many conifers, these shrubs are often used in formal gardens. They maintain their shape without the need for frequent pruning.

Low branching   The lowest branches of these shrubs reach, or nearly reach, the ground. They can be used as a filler for low-maintenance areas.

Roundheaded   Often used as a specimen, these give a casual, natural look to the landscape.

Prostrate or spreading   Best suited for use as ground covers, these shrubs have branches that either grow horizontally or are weak and lie on the ground.

Columnar   The branches of these shrubs angle upward sharply, keeping their outline narrow. Use them for dramatic emphasis in the landscape.

Sheared boxwood (Buxus) hedges define the outline of this peaceful formal garden.

Many subtle variations in form and color can exist among varieties within a shrub species. Seen here are Hinoki false-cypress (Chamaecyparis obtusa), right, and Lawson false-cypress (Chamaecyparis lawsoniana), left.

Compact or dense The leaves of these shrubs grow close together, giving them a dense, opaque appearance. Their compact shape makes them useful as a screen, blocking the view from one part of the garden to another.

Open These shrubs can be seen through, making the framework of their branches visible. Many are useful as specimen plants.

Weeping Although the stems and branches are strong, new twigs are weak and bend toward the ground. Use shrubs of this shape for a solemn, graceful touch.

A plant can be pruned and trained into almost any shape the owner desires. However, directing a plant's growth into a shape other than its natural form creates ongoing maintenance work. Select shrubs that naturally grow into forms that work with the design.

When selecting a shrub for a particular use, choose according to its mature height. In general, shrubs that grow to be under 1 foot are best suited for use as ground covers; those up to 1½ feet form low hedges; and those that grow to 3 feet provide an effective barrier to traffic. Shrubs that reach 6 feet can be used for privacy without giving a sense of being walled in. Those growing to 8 feet can form windbreaks or be used as background planting. Shrubs that exceed 8 feet when mature are most effective in large gardens, where they can serve many of the same purposes as small trees—as a wind screen, as background for other plantings, or as a specimen.

DESIGNING WITH SHRUBS

The design basics discussed here will help in making most general design decisions. When creating an entirely new landscape or making a major change in an existing garden, refer to Ortho's book *All About Landscaping,* which details garden design and construction from beginning to end.

The two ends of the landscape design spectrum are formal and informal. Although the choice of plants is important in creating these styles, the same plants can be used to create either a formal or an informal design. The overall style of a garden is established in large part by the lines, shapes, spaces, and enclosures of the design, in addition to the horticultural groupings. Plants, materials, and structures are chosen to complement and enhance the desired effect.

Balanced Plantings

Good design in either a formal or informal garden requires balance. The balance in a formal garden seems obvious in its straight lines and symmetrical, rectangular forms, although there may be more to it than immediately meets the eye. The balance in an informal garden, where plants are more natural in form, is

not as obvious but is every bit as important. Balance leads to a sense of continuity between different kinds of plants. No matter what the garden style, balance can be achieved in a variety of ways.

☐ Plant taller-growing varieties behind shorter-growing ones. Although design rules need to be flexible, they should not be broken without thought. There's no sense in planting short plants behind tall ones unless the tall ones will be kept severely pruned.

☐ Place plants with lighter foliage in front of those with darker foliage. While dark-leafed plants can be placed in front of light ones, the effect is not as dramatic. The arrangement of light leaves in front of dark leaves is more pleasing. Sun on light-colored leaves against a dark backdrop is particularly striking.

☐ Select background plants for their dark foliage, their base-branching form, and their leaf texture. Background plants should provide a suitable backdrop for the more showy plants in front. Background plants often perform the same function as hedges, but are not pruned as regularly and are allowed to reach greater heights. To minimize confusion, make

a background out of the same variety or two similar varieties in an alternating pattern.

☐ Limit the number of plant varieties, used as background and throughout the garden. Use what grows well in your climate and particular situation. Grouping together plants of one variety makes a stronger design statement than planting many individual specimens of assorted, unrelated varieties. Once the framework of your design is in place, a few well-selected accents can add a great deal of interest and variety. A garden with a few selected varieties and occasional accents will have an organized, purposeful look while still providing visual interest.

Color

Most people only think of flowers when they think of color in the garden. Although flowers, including flowering shrubs, may present the most obvious color, shrub foliage can also provide many striking variations of color. For example, there are so many shades of green foliage that it would be almost impossible to go to a nursery and pick out five different shrubs of an identical color.

Besides the many hues of green, shrubs have gray, red, purple, yellow, and variegated foliage that can be used effectively in contrast to green. The seasons also bring many different, changing colors—the bare bark and branches of winter, the bright new growth and flowering of spring, the more muted tones of summer, and the fruits and changing foliage of fall.

Some gardeners like the understatement of an all-green garden; others want more variety. Before selecting a shrub, consider your preferences for a seasonal show—do you want a display of green, or other colors as well? Consider that in those parts of the country that have extended winters, shrubs with colorful bark and twigs, persistent fruit, and interesting leaf texture may actually be evident in the garden for as much of the year as those with flowers and green leaves. When choosing flowering shrubs, find out what colors the flowers are and when they bloom. Then plot their locations so that the colors will complement each other rather than clash. This formula applies to foliage, too. Try to imagine in advance whether a new shrub with gray-green leaves, for example, will look attractive with an existing shrub with yellow leaves.

In selecting foliage color, avoid accentuating problems that surrounding plants may have. For example, yellow-leafed plants would draw unwanted attention to shrubs that are prone to yellowing caused by iron deficiency, such as citrus or gardenia.

Texture

When selecting shrubs, notice the different textures produced by a shrub's leaf size and pattern and by its bare branches, twigs, and bark during the dormant season. Are the leaves small and compact, giving a neat, clipped appearance? Or are they large and uneven, creating a bold, informal feeling? Do the leaves have a coarse or fine pattern to them? What does the shrub look like in winter?

Judge the texture of a plant close up, then look at it again from 40 feet away. Does the texture still look the same? Some shrubs lose their pleasing effect when they are planted too far away. Conversely, the texture of a large-leafed shrub may be out of scale when it is planted in a confined space or where viewing it up close is the only option.

shrub may be its form, flowers, berries, shape, color, texture, or rarity, as well as its personal significance. The number of specimens used in a single landscape is usually limited to one or two—any more than that and the special quality would be diminished.

To be fully appreciated, specimen plants should be placed where they are most visible in the garden. For example, if a specimen's unique features need close viewing, place the plant by the front door or walkway so that it receives the attention it deserves.

Compatibility

Planning, time, and care are necessary to achieve a pleasing, balanced planting of shrubs. Although a shrub can be moved relatively easily within a year or two of planting, once it is planted it generally will be in the ground a long time.

When buying more than one shrub, arrange them together in one place at the nursery in the way they will appear in the garden. How do they look together? Do their textures, forms, and colors complement each other? Some diversity is necessary to create interest. For example, a dark green, needled evergreen shrub may look particularly attractive when placed near a finely textured, light green broad-leafed shrub.

When adding new shrubs to established plantings, take samples of the existing plants to the nursery. While selecting new plants, consider the garden as it is now. Will the additions be appropriate, creating an interesting, balanced scene?

Taking the time to consider these elements of design not only will increase your appreciation of the unique qualities of shrubs, but also will result in a landscape that most matches your chosen design.

Plant Spacing

How close should two plants be placed in a garden? This depends on how important the final effect is to your scheme. If screening is needed immediately, plant shrubs close together. For an entryway, the added cost of additional shrubs might be worth the benefit of handsome, closely knit foliage. Inquire at the local garden center to learn the best spacings of shrubs.

One general rule is to plant finely textured plants in front of coarsely textured varieties. The combined pattern of graduated textures is pleasing. If a dramatic effect is intended, choose coarsely textured, large-leafed shrubs. If a more tailored, formal landscape is desired, select compact shrubs with comparatively small leaves. Many of the conifers can contribute to the formal effect, depending on how they are used.

Special Effects

Many different effects can be achieved by using unique shrubs known as specimen plants. They usually have some feature or combination of features that sets them apart from other shrubs. The uniqueness of a specimen

PRACTICAL CONSIDERATIONS

In designing the garden, keep in mind that shrubs can be practical as well as attractive. By shielding the yard from wind, hiding an unattractive area, or masking an oddly shaped building, you can improve the general environment in your garden. Here are some of the ways in which shrubs and hedges can do double duty.

Wind Control

A windbreak should be placed on the side of the yard from which the prevailing winter wind blows. Windbreaks may be required on more than one side, depending upon the orientation of the property. A single hedgerow of shrubs can be effective, but a double row, planted on staggered centers, creates a baffle that is even better at stopping the wind.

This hedge forms a baffle, protecting a vegetable garden and patio from the wind.

Shrubs and hedges are used in many ways to modify the architectural shapes of this house: as foundation plantings, for color and symmetry, and as a visual interruption to the long brick stairway.

Wind Control

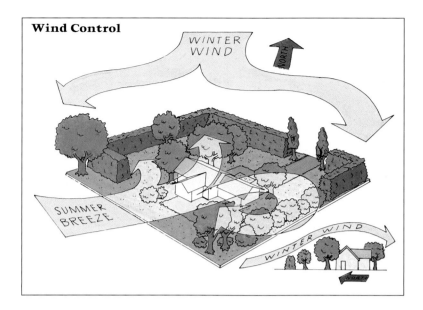

Traffic Control

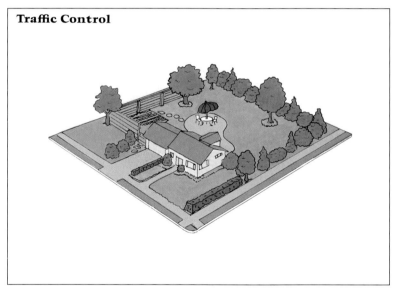

Privacy

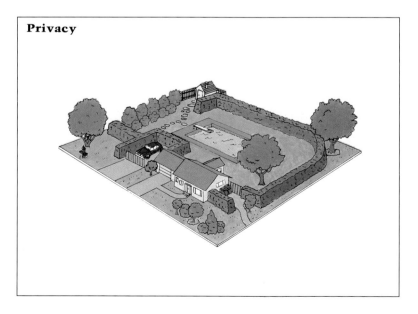

Maximum wind reduction occurs within a space of from four to seven times the height of the windbreak. Using this calculation, a hedge that will eventually grow 6 feet high should be planted, at the most, 24 to 42 feet away from the area you want to protect from the wind. Carefully planned windbreaks can both deflect cold winter winds and capture and direct cooling summer breezes.

Dust Reduction

A solid row of shrubs can considerably reduce the amount of dust. Larger pieces of debris are also trapped by shrubs, keeping them from spoiling your yard. If you live in a dusty, sooty area, select pollution-resistant species and spray the leaves of barrier plantings with water to keep them healthy. A list of shrubs suitable for city dwellers is included in the "Plant Selection Guide" on page 51.

Barriers and Traffic Control

Shrubs can be well used to both keep people out of areas where you don't want them and guide them to areas where you do.

When planning to use shrubs as guides or barriers, think of them as architectural forms rather than as plants. Select barrier plants for their density and sturdiness. For example, to keep people out of certain areas, choose thorny or prickly plants. See the list of thorny barrier shrubs on page 59. These types of shrubs also work well under windows to deter prowlers. The shrub must grow tightly against the house; an access space between the house and the shrub could aid a prowler by acting as a protective screen.

Architectural Elements

Carefully placed shrubs can help disguise unattractive features of a home—unbalanced proportions, oddly shaped windows, tall foundation walls, or other architectural imbalances. Custom corrections of this kind can make a big difference for a relatively small investment of time and money.

As with all plant selection, choose the right shrubs for your purpose. Consider what form is needed to correct a proportion problem or to balance out a poorly placed window. It may be helpful to take a photograph of the house, sketch in the shape that is needed, and bring it to the local garden center for suggestions.

Planning, Buying, and Planting

Careful planning before buying and planting shrubs will help you make the best choices. Select healthy plants and follow proper planting techniques.

No matter what style you choose for your garden, the most attractive landscape is one filled with plants that are vigorous and healthy. Your plants will be vigorous and healthy if they receive proper care and are planted in a suitable environment. The importance of matching a plant's needs with the conditions of a particular spot in your yard cannot be overemphasized.

A shrub may look attractive in a catalog, nursery, or friend's garden, but learn about the plant's needs and character before choosing it for your own home. Does it need full sun, filtered shade, or morning sun? In what kind of soil does it grow best? What are the water requirements? Be certain that the plant will grow in the locations you have in mind. Talk with nursery staff about plant requirements, or take descriptions of shrubs—such as the ones found in the "Plant Selection Guide" on page 51—with you to the garden center.

Not all shrubs have strict cultural and climatic requirements. With proper care, shrubs tolerate a wide range of conditions. If the conditions don't naturally occur, you can make modifications that change the site. The following pages give specifics on how to change the growing conditions to suit the particular needs of the plant, as well as information on the various ways plants are packaged for sale. This chapter also contains instructions for planting shrubs brought home from the nursery, transplanting shrubs from one location to another, and planting shrubs in containers for mobility and garden versatility.

Choosing shrubs that meet your design and practical needs, selecting healthy plants, and planting them properly are all essential for a successful garden.

SOIL

In general, shrubs are very adaptable plants. Given the proper care, they will grow well in most soils. However, knowing about and working with the type of soil you have will help ensure healthy plants. Most soils fall into a large middle range that provides a healthy environment for plants. Where the soil is outside that middle range, it is necessary to select plants adapted to the soil or to determine what steps can be taken to improve the soil. Although there are many exceptions to soil guidelines, the following general comments will help you make use of the extensive information available on this important gardening subject.

Soils are classified according to their depth, fertility, texture, and structure. An ideal garden soil has a topsoil that is several feet deep; is reasonably fertile; has a balanced texture composed of sand, silt, and clay particles; and has a structure with enough air space between particles to promote both good drainage and water retention. In addition, the ideal soil has an acid-to-alkaline balance conducive to the healthy growth of most plants.

Very few soils are absolutely ideal. In most cases, however, there are relatively simple ways to improve soils. Furthermore, because of the complex nature of soil, when one aspect is improved, other problems are often eliminated as well.

The most accurate way to find out what kind of soil you have is to have samples of it tested in a soil laboratory. For more information on soil testing, call your local county extension agent and find out whether your state offers a soil testing program.

Testing for fertility is not easy, so many gardeners choose to add a complete fertilizer to the soil at prescribed intervals during the growing season to make up for any deficiencies the soil may have.

Loam soils have the best texture of all garden soils, but both sandy and clay soils can be improved with the addition of organic matter. The organic matter may be compost, rotted manure, nitrogen-stabilized bark or sawdust, ground corncobs, or other locally available material. Organic matter can be added to the entire yard or just to the areas about to receive new shrubs. The one rule to follow with organic matter is to be sure to add enough.

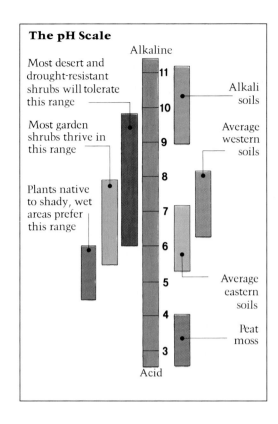

The pH Scale

Alkaline

Most desert and drought-resistant shrubs will tolerate this range

Most garden shrubs thrive in this range

Plants native to shady, wet areas prefer this range

Alkali soils

Average western soils

Average eastern soils

Peat moss

Acid

One third to one half of the final mixed soil should be organic matter. This means that if you cultivate to a depth of 8 inches, add 3 to 4 inches of organic matter over the top of the soil before mixing it in.

The way in which a soil drains is determined by its structure—the way soil particles are held together. The same methods that work to improve the texture of the soil are also effective in improving its structure, which in turn helps drainage. Whether there is too much air space, as in sandy soils, or too little, as in clay soils, the addition of organic matter helps to correct the problem.

MICROCLIMATES

Microclimates are small, specific areas of distinct climate conditions within a residential lot. The positions of buildings, fences, slopes, and vegetation all contribute to the creation of the microclimates in your yard. Knowing and using or modifying existing microclimates allows you to select the right shrub for the right spot. For example, shrubs able to grow on the north, cooler side of the house would probably find conditions on the warmer south side intolerable. Before buying any new shrubs, take an inventory of the microclimates in your yard.

Your house is a constant climate regulator, with almost perpetual shade on the north side, full sun and the most heat radiation to the south, half shade and hot sun to the west, and half shade and milder sun on the east side. The walls themselves radiate heat to varying degrees, and roof overhangs conserve outgoing radiated heat, making it warmer under the eaves on frosty nights. With those basics in mind, you can assess areas in your yard and match them with plant requirements.

CLIMATE MODIFICATION

Once you know what microclimates exist in your garden, you may find a need to change them. Here are some pointers for increasing or decreasing certain climate characteristics.

To Increase Heat

☐ Plan for maximum flat surfaces—paved areas, patios, untilled ground, rock, or masonry areas. These surfaces absorb large amounts of the sun's radiation and, in turn, give off heat to surrounding areas.

☐ Plan for a "ceiling" in your yard, such as a patio cover or an overhead lath, which traps the warm air that reradiates from other surfaces at night.

☐ Plant or build windbreaks and cold-air diverters. Cold air sinks to the lowest part of the yard. If you can divert the path of cold air with a hedge or fence, you can keep the shielded area warmer.

☐ Plan sun pockets that trap the sun on cool spring mornings. A two-sided fence or screen can create a warm climate that is radically different from the rest of your yard.

To Reduce Heat

☐ Grow vines on overhead structures and plant shade trees.

☐ Plant bare soil with ground covers, lawns, or other plants. Bare soil can deflect summer heat, which can raise the temperature of adjoining areas.

☐ Prune the lower growth of trees and large shrubs for increased air circulation and cooler temperatures.

Although garden climates may be modified to make them more hospitable for plants, selecting the right plant for the right place is equally important. These azaleas thrive in the shade of an oak.

To Reduce Wind

☐ Plant or build windbreaks, baffles, or diverters. For the best placement of hedges and fences, see the information on pages 14 and 15.

☐ Make semienclosed outdoor living areas with fences and solid overhead coverings.

Top: When selecting a container shrub, check to be sure the container and plant sizes are proportionate. Here are 1-gallon and 5-gallon containers.
Bottom: Check the soil, roots, foliage color, and overall balance of a container shrub before purchasing.

To Increase Humidity

☐ Plan for thick overhead vegetation, which slows evaporation and adds water through transpiration.

☐ Use plenty of ground covers.

☐ Add a pool or fountain.

To Reduce Humidity

☐ Provide maximum ventilation by pruning trees and shrubs in an open manner.

☐ Make sure the drainage of the entire yard is good so that there is no standing water in any spot.

☐ Make maximum use of paved or decked areas that, as flat surfaces, encourage drying winds.

BUYING SHRUBS

Shrubs are most commonly sold in containers. The containers may be metal, plastic, fiber, or wood, and are available in many sizes. Most shrubs are planted in 1- gallon or 5-gallon containers. Specimen shrubs are sometimes sold in 15-gallon containers.

The decision of which size to buy depends upon how long you are willing to wait for the shrub to grow to ideal proportions. In selecting a shrub, consider that it takes approximately 1½ to 2 years for a 1-gallon-sized shrub to

Check the Root System

If the plant moves up and down in the soil, the roots are not well established.

Thick, circling, exposed roots indicate the container is too small and the plant is pot-bound.

Unwrap the burlap and check the rootball—a broken rootball indicates root damage.

An oversized plant in a small can is sure to be root-bound, or has possibly sent its roots past the can, down into the soil below. In either case, the plant should be avoided.

Shrubs in plastic cans can be slipped out easily without doing any damage to the root system, with the added bonus that the plastic container can be reused. Metal cans have to be cut in order to get the plant out. Large specimen shrubs in wooden containers must have the container dismantled before planting.

Check the container Make sure the container is in good shape when you purchase the shrub. Rusted metal cans, split plastic, or disintegrated wood usually mean that the roots of the plant have grown into the ground soil at the nursery. Taking the plant away from its accustomed site may cause it severe shock.

Check the branches The shrub branches should be evenly spaced, indicating that the plant has had continuous growth under good growing conditions. New shoot growth should be uniform all the way around the plant. This indicates that the plant has a fully developed, balanced root system. Foliage growth should be balanced and vigorous.

reach 5-gallon size. In 2½ to 3 years, shrubs starting out in both 1-gallon and 5-gallon containers will be about the same size.

Choosing a Container Plant

When selecting a shrub, be sure it matches the size of its container. A small plant in a 5-gallon can is as poor a buy as a large plant in a 1-gallon can, but for different reasons. The small plant in the 5-gallon container may have been recently moved from a 1-gallon can. In effect, you are paying a 5-gallon price for a 1-gallon plant. Although nurseries must transplant 1-gallon stock into 5-gallon containers as it grows larger, these transplants should be held in a growing area until they reach 5-gallon size.

Plants that have recently been repotted into larger containers may be recognized by the relatively small size of the plant, a small rootball indicating a smaller root system, and by the soil in the container being unusually soft and loose, because it has not yet been packed down by repeated waterings.

Inspecting Shrub Branches

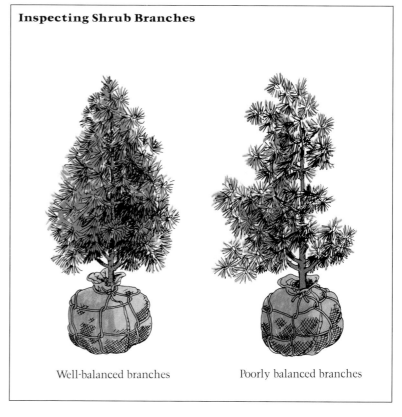

Well-balanced branches   Poorly balanced branches

Check pruning cuts   Make sure there are no signs of recent severe cutting back. All pruning cuts should be made down to outside buds so that the plant will keep its natural shape and not grow crisscrossed branches. There shouldn't be any short stubs left from pruning, as these invite disease and insect attacks as they die back.

Check the root system   The shrub should be well anchored in the container, but not to the point of being root-bound. Try gently lifting the plant by the trunk; if the soil moves at all, the plant has not had time to develop roots throughout the rootball.

If the plant has been in the container too long, growth will have stopped and will be difficult to start again. Check for thick masses of roots on the soil surface or around all the sides of the soil ball. Without careful pruning and straightening, the roots will go on growing in the same circle and never expand into the garden soil. Plants with confined root systems struggle to survive in a small area of soil—the size of the original container—and may topple in heavy winds.

Balled-and-Burlapped Shrubs

Balled-and-burlapped shrubs can be bought and planted any time, but spring is the preferred season. Polyethylene and other synthetic materials are often used in place of burlap; the guidelines for handling are the

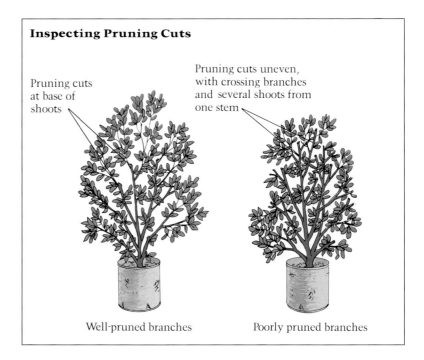

Inspecting Pruning Cuts

Pruning cuts at base of shoots

Pruning cuts uneven, with crossing branches and several shoots from one stem

Well-pruned branches   Poorly pruned branches

same for both. The advantage of burlap is that it rots readily and can be left under the shrub when you plant it (see page 27). Synthetic material must be removed before planting as it does not rot and can cause the plant to become root-bound.

To pick a balled-and-burlapped plant, untie the wrapping material and look carefully at the rootball. It should have a well-developed network of small, fibrous roots. Don't choose a shrub with a ball of soil that is loose, cracked, broken, or bone dry.

A Mexican-orange (Choisya ternata) in a 1-gallon plastic container (left) and a balled-and-burlapped azalea (right) show two of the most common ways plants are available for sale.

Buying Bare-Root Plants

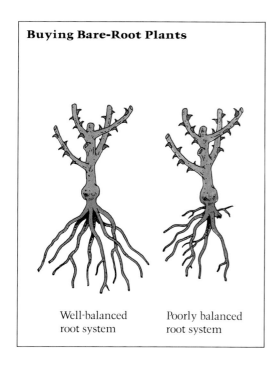

Well-balanced root system

Poorly balanced root system

Roses are most commonly purchased as bare-root plants.

After you select the shrub that you want, retie the wrapping material and carry it from the bottom of the rootball—don't use the trunk as a handle. Balled-and-burlapped plants are top heavy and not very stable. To keep them from falling over, tie or lean them against a wall or fence. Until planting, store the shrub in the shade, and keep the rootball moist by watering slowly from the top. In warm weather, wet the foliage occasionally as well.

Bare-Root Shrubs

Bare-root shrubs are less expensive than container plants and tend to establish themselves more rapidly because they do not have to make the transition from nursery container soil to your garden soil. They are only available during the dormant season, and they should always be planted before growth begins. For the best selection, shop at the beginning of the bare-root season, in late winter or early spring. Many varieties of deciduous shrubs are available in bare-root form, particularly roses and shrubs commonly used as hedge plants.

Before buying a bare-root shrub, carefully examine its root system. Look for several good-sized, brown roots going in different directions at different levels from the main root. In most cases the upper part of the plant should be pruned before it leaves the nursery. If you are unable to plant the shrub right

Dwarf Shrubs

The trend toward smaller property lots for both urban and suburban homes, coupled with a rising demand for plants that are easy to maintain, has resulted in more and more dwarf shrubs being offered for sale in nurseries.

Dwarf shrubs can have many origins. Some, like heather (*Calluna vulgaris*), are naturally low growing. Many of these plants have evolved under harsh environmental conditions where survival favored dwarfs that could evade cold and drying winds. Other dwarfs have been bred using a variety of horticultural techniques.

Regardless of their origin, the dwarfs are very useful in garden design. Where garden space is at a premium, they are ideal. The unusual character of many dwarf varieties commonly causes them to be used only as specimens, but they can be integrated and blended as well as the larger forms. Dwarfs are excellent in foundation plantings, where their slow, restrained growth provides an easy-care answer to the transition from vertical walls to horizontal lawns and beds. Many dwarf shrubs stay low

but spread wide and are a good choice for difficult steep banks. Others have restrained growth in all directions that makes them a perfect choice for edging along drives, walks, borders, and beds—anywhere, in fact, that a neat, low, formal or informal hedge or demarcation is desired.

The slow-growing habit of dwarf shrubs can make them easier to care for in the landscape. Pruning and shearing need to be done much less frequently, and feeding requirements are usually fewer. For those dwarf shrubs that are propagated from side branches or juvenile growth parts, special care must be taken to ensure that they do not revert to their more vigorous, upright antecedents. Immediately remove any branches that exhibit a larger growth habit or foliage. This is particularly a problem with some forms of *Euonymus*, false-cypress, and juniper. Avoid overfeeding slow-growing dwarfs; they need less fertilizer than their forebears. Generally, the care of dwarf shrubs is the same as that for their larger form. See the list beginning on page 62 for a selection of dwarf shrubs.

When planting hedge shrubs, space them so they will fill in gaps when mature.

away, cover the roots with sawdust or damp earth to keep them from drying out. Dried roots quickly lose their ability to continue growing. Store the plants in a cool place to keep the buds from opening too early.

SELECTING HEDGE PLANTS

The deciduous plants commonly used for hedges are often available as bare-root plants. One of the most popular hedge shrubs is the privet (*Ligustrum*). There are many varieties of privet; those offered at the local garden center most likely are best adapted to your climate. Good-quality bare-root privets are usually from 12 to 24 inches tall, with sturdy stems and well-developed root systems.

If no bare-root plants are available at the time you want to start your hedge, buy plants in 1-gallon-sized containers. The largest plant is not always the best buy, considering that the plant must be heavily pruned to force as many new shoots as possible from the base. Look for vigorous plants that are well branched.

Slow-growing evergreen shrubs, such as yew (*Taxus*), holly (*Ilex*), and the various varieties of boxwood (*Buxus*) are among the most preferred varieties for hedges. Although they are slow growing, they develop into a denser hedge that needs less pruning than some faster-growing choices, such as privet.

If you want a neatly trimmed hedge, consider that plants with large leaves demand more specialized care than smaller-leafed varieties. For example, the English laurel (*Prunus laurocerasus*) is an attractive broad-leafed evergreen shrub sometimes used for hedges. The large size of its leaves, however, demands that a hedge of English laurel be pruned selectively rather than sheared. Shearing plants with oversized leaves causes an abundance of imperfect, cut-up leaves.

BRINGING PLANTS HOME

Because cut metal cans are difficult to water correctly, have a can cut at the nursery only if you are going to plant the shrub that same day. Don't attempt to bring a shrub home in a car in which the plant does not comfortably fit. Plants can become rapidly windburned if left exposed in a speeding automobile. If you must take your new shrub home with you, protect it by wrapping it securely in cloth or some other protective material. Many nurseries and garden centers will deliver purchases free of charge. Take advantage of this service, and both you and your new plant will benefit.

PLANTING

The best planting methods for shrubs have remained essentially the same for centuries. However, recent changes in nursery methods have resulted in modifications of these techniques, and research continues to add to our knowledge about planting.

Transition Soil

Most shrubs adapt well to the large middle range of native soils available to most gardeners. However, nursery shrubs are grown in a lightweight, porous growing medium formulated to keep the plants healthy while they are in their containers, and shrubs go through a period of transition as they grow accustomed to the garden soil. Although plants that start out in transition soil—backfill soil to which amendments have been added—do better than other plants at first, after five years they are not as healthy as ones planted with unamended backfill soil. The best solution is to select plants that are particularly adapted to your soil.

The Planting Steps

The steps outlined below will help to ensure healthy, well-adapted shrubs. The steps described are for shrubs bought in containers. The procedures for planting bare-root and for planting balled-and-burlapped plants are essentially the same; the differences between them are discussed on pages 27 and 28.

Almost any time of year is fine to plant shrubs, as long as the soil is workable and the planting time doesn't immediately precede a period that may cause the shrub stress. If a spade or cultivator cannot be used easily in the soil, wait until the soil dries out. Late spring and late fall are usually the least favorable times for planting as the approaching heat or cold can place newly established plants under stress.

Dig the planting hole Dig a hole approximately twice as wide and slightly shallower than the rootball. Plants have a tendency to sink after planting, so they may suffer from crown and root rot if the hole is dug deeper than the rootball. The rootball should be sitting on firm, undisturbed soil.

Amend and fertilize the backfill soil If you've decided to place the shrub in a transition soil (see above), now is the time to amend the soil. Keep the backfill soil—the soil taken from the planting hole—in a pile and roughly estimate its volume. Next, add some slow-decomposition organic soil amendment. Approximately 25 percent of the final mix should be soil amendment.

The Planting Steps

Follow these steps to ensure the healthy transition of a shrub from container to ground.

- ☐ Dig the planting hole
- ☐ Amend and fertilize the backfill soil
- ☐ Remove shrub from container
- ☐ Place shrub in the hole
- ☐ Fill hole and build a basin
- ☐ Prune
- ☐ Water

Digging a hole is the first step in planting.

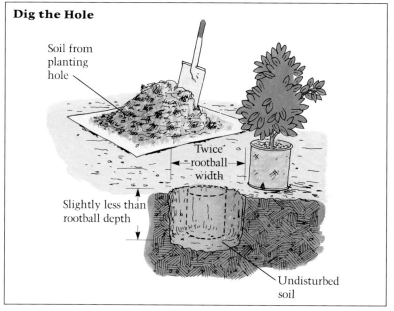

Dig the Hole

Soil from planting hole

Twice rootball width

Slightly less than rootball depth

Undisturbed soil

When planting a new shrub in early spring or when leaf growth is about to begin, add a complete fertilizer to the backfill soil. For dry fertilizers, 1 to 2 tablespoons is adequate for 1-gallon container shrubs, and ¼ cup for plants in 5-gallon containers. For whatever fertilizer you select, follow the manufacturer's instructions carefully. Stir the fertilizer into the soil to prevent the rootball from coming into direct contact with unmixed fertilizer.

Remove shrub from container Shrubs grown in plastic or sleeve-type containers slip out easily, especially if the rootball is damp. Keep the rootball intact—a broken rootball can permanently damage the root system. If the shrub is in a metal can and you are going

Amend Backfill Soil

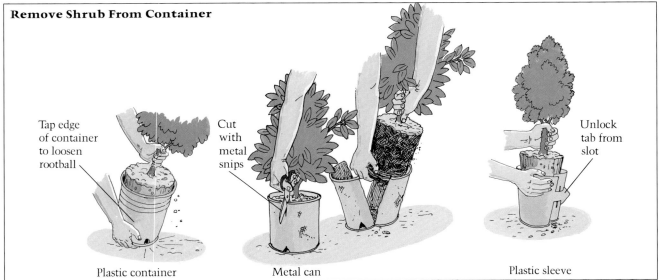

Remove Shrub From Container

Tap edge of container to loosen rootball

Cut with metal snips

Unlock tab from slot

Plastic container   Metal can   Plastic sleeve

to plant the shrub the same day you buy it, ask a nursery worker to cut the container. If the shrub will not be planted the same day, leave the can intact. When ready to plant, cut the can using a large pair of metal snips or a can cutter like the type used at the nursery. Be careful not to cut or damage the rootball.

Place shrub in the hole Before placing the shrub in the hole, check the rootball. Cut or pull away any circled, matted, or tangled roots so that the roots radiate out from the rootball. Matted roots often stay compacted and do not extend into the surrounding soil. Compensate for any damaged or cut roots by lightly trimming the top of the shrub and place the shrub in the hole.

Place Shrub in Hole

Loosen roots with knife or metal snips

Fill the Hole and Build a Basin

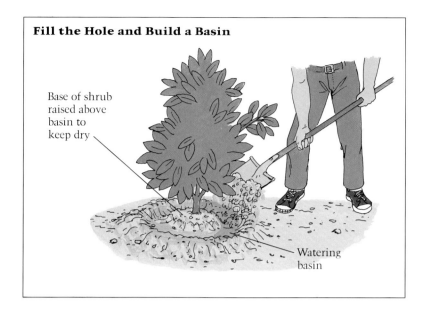

Base of shrub raised above basin to keep dry

Watering basin

Prune

Prune as necessary to balance shape and form of shrub

Planting Balled-and-Burlapped Shrubs

If not biodegradable, remove wrapping and string from rootball

Fill hole and build a basin   Fill the hole with backfill soil to the level of the surrounding soil. Build a shallow basin around the shrub so that irrigation water will be concentrated in the area where it is needed most. Build the basin so that the stem of the plant will remain dry—wet stems are susceptible to rot. Thoroughly water the soil around the root zone. Apply water until the soil is loose and muddy. Gently jiggle the plant to eliminate any remaining air pockets and settle the plant into the hole. Check to be sure that water drains away from the stem of the plant.

Use the basin for watering until some roots have had a chance to expand into the surrounding soil, usually within 6 weeks. If dry weather conditions require continued irrigation, enlarge the basin as necessary. Break down the basin once the plant is established.

Prune   Shrubs planted from containers rarely require pruning immediately after planting, except for cosmetic purposes. See the chapter on pruning (page 41) for methods appropriate to the particular kind of shrub.

Water   Watch the shrub closely to see how much water it requires. If a newly planted shrub wilts during the hottest part of the day, the rootball is not getting enough water, even though the surrounding soil may appear wet. Even if it rains or if the plant is reached by a sprinkler, it may need to be watered by hand two to three times a week for the first few weeks if the soil seems dry. Do not overwater—too much water is as bad as too little.

Planting Balled-and-Burlapped Shrubs

In addition to the steps described above for planting shrubs from containers, balled-and-burlapped shrubs require some further procedures to thrive.

Handle the ball carefully, setting it in the hole with the wrap still on. Adjust the height of the rootball, as you would with a shrub from a container. If the burlap has been treated to retard rotting or if the wrap is made of a nonbiodegradable material (ask at the nursery), remove it before planting.

For shrubs wrapped in biodegradable material, untie the material and pull it away from the top of the rootball. If the strings pull

Planting Bare-Root Shrubs

Top of roots 1″ below surface of soil

Work backfill soil between roots to remove air pockets

away easily, discard them; if not, leave them to rot in the soil. Remove synthetic twine, which does not rot. Cut or fold the wrap back so that it is below the surface of the soil—exposed material acts like a wick and draws water out of the soil.

Prune as necessary to compensate for the roots that were lost when the shrub was dug up by the grower. A little extra fertilizer and water will compensate for any roots that were pruned away earlier.

Planting Bare-Root Shrubs

Nurseries usually prune bare-root shrubs for the customer after pulling them from the holding bed. Pruning the bare roots—sometimes one third or more—results in a stronger shrub.

Store bare-root shrubs in a cool spot with their roots in moist sawdust or bark to prevent them from drying out until ready to plant. Dig a hole large enough to accommodate the full span of the roots. Prune off any broken or very long roots, and place the plant in the hole with the top root 1 inch below the level of the surrounding soil. Work the backfill soil between the roots with your hands, to remove any air pockets.

Because bare-root shrubs are always planted while they are dormant, it is not necessary to add fertilizer. Unlike other plants, a bare-root shrub probably does not need watering again until the spring (see the planting illustration above).

Planting Hedges

Hedge shrubs can be planted either in a trench or in individual holes. Although the methods are interchangeable, the trench method generally works best for bare-root plantings, and the individual hole method works best for plants from containers. The planting steps described above apply for either method.

Single-Row Trench Method   Double-Row Trench Method

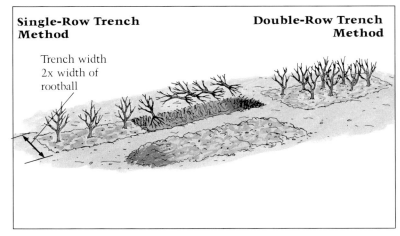

Trench width 2x width of rootball

Individual Hole Method

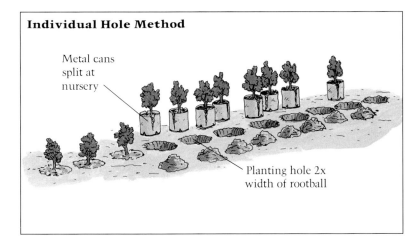

Metal cans split at nursery

Planting hole 2x width of rootball

Double Hole Method

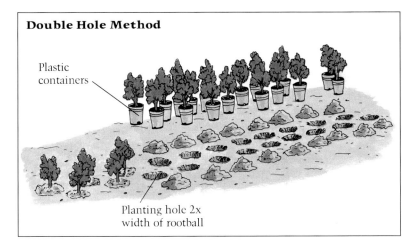

Plastic containers

Planting hole 2x width of rootball

The width of the trench should be twice the width of the rootball. A double, staggered row of shrubs results in the more rapid growth of a thicker, denser, and wider hedge, but involves twice the initial expense and effort. When planting a double row, stagger the plants so that no two plants are directly opposite each other.

The best spacing between individual plants depends both upon the potential branch spread of the shrub variety and upon how rapidly you want the hedge to fill in. Spacing can be from 18 inches to 30 inches apart. Most gardeners recommend a spacing of 18 to 20 inches within the row to avoid root crowding. Some dwarf varieties are planted 12 inches apart. Ask at your nursery for advice on particular varieties (see illustrations on page 28).

TRANSPLANTING

Transplanting involves moving an established shrub from one spot in the garden to a new one. Transplanting is a useful design tool as it allows the garden to be adjusted as it matures. Transplanting any shrub, whether large or small, represents some danger to the plant. The worst problems are caused by root loss, either because some of the roots are broken off while the shrub is being dug out of the ground or because the rootball is allowed to dry out before the shrub is safely placed in its new location.

Transplanting Small Shrubs

For the purpose of transplanting, a small shrub can be defined as one that can be carried on a shovel or spade after it has been dug. The first step is to dig the hole in the new location (see page 25). Next, with a sharp spade, cut around the entire shrub you want to transplant. On the last downward cut, tip the spade back and gently lift the shrub out. Carry the shrub on the spade to the new location. Next, follow the steps described on pages 25 to 27 for planting a new shrub. See illustrations at right.

Transplanting Large Shrubs

The first step in transplanting a large shrub is to have the new hole ready to receive the plant. Next, prune away or tie up the low branches of the shrub to permit easy access to its base. Dig a ditch around the plant. Using a

Tips for Transplanting

Transplanting small and large shrubs requires some special care and preparation.

☐ Transplant during cool, moist weather—roots dry out quickly on warm, windy days. Just before transplanting, spray both broad-leafed and coniferous evergreens with an antitranspirant, a chemical that prevents leaves from losing water through transpiration.

☐ Move a shrub when it is dormant or as inactive as possible.

☐ Dig around the root system to create as large a rootball as you can handle to minimize root loss, and be careful not to break it. The soil should be fairly moist but not muddy. If roots are lost during digging, compensate by pruning the top of the shrub by the same proportion that is lost from the root system.

☐ Prune plant tips rather than thinning out a lean skeleton.

☐ Spray or mist the foliage. Due to root loss or damage during transplanting, plants may wilt in the hot sun.

Transplanting Small Shrubs

Cut roots on all sides with a sharp spade

Place shrub in prepared hole

sharp shovel, undercut the rootball from one side until the shrub is about to topple over. Have a piece of burlap ready—a gunnysack cut so that it spreads open works well—and push it down evenly on the undercut side. Continue digging on the opposite side until it is possible to topple the shrub onto the burlap. Wrap the burlap around the rootball and tie with twine to keep the rootball together. Lift the shrub onto a piece of heavy plastic so that you can slide the shrub to its new location, or put it on a wheelbarrow or hand truck. Plant according to the instructions for balled-and-burlapped shrubs on page 27. See illustrations of the process below.

Transplanting Large Shrubs

Prune lower branches

Dig a ditch around the rootball

Cut under the rootball on one side

Tuck burlap beneath the rootball

Pull burlap under the rootball

Rootball wrapped in burlap

Slide shrub to new location on sheet of plastic

Growing Shrubs in Containers

Planting a shrub in a container gives it a singular importance that can turn it into a prized specimen. Shrubs in containers often turn out to be the showpieces of the garden, and the extra attention they demand and receive often results in spectacular plants. See the list of shrubs that do well in containers beginning on page 58.

Practical Benefits

Besides the specimen qualities they achieve, shrubs planted in containers also have practical benefits. They can be moved from one location in the garden to another, or from one home to another. Shrubs that won't grow in the local soil can be placed in containers with suitably amended soil. Those that won't survive the extremes of the local climate can be moved to protected areas as necessary. In addition, container shrubs are an easy and flexible way to make a patio or entranceway attractive. Blooming container shrubs can provide seasonal, portable color to a garden.

Size and Growth

The intermediate size of most shrubs makes them good candidates for container culture. Many familiar shrubs grown in the open ground—such as wisteria, boxwood, or lilac—grow well in containers.

Although any shrub can be grown in a container, the best choices are those that are relatively slow growing and have a compact habit. Fast-growing shrubs need to be repotted more often and require more pruning. Because of their naturally small size, dwarf shrubs are ideal subjects for container culture. See page 23 for information on dwarf shrubs and page 62 for a list of recommendations.

Hardiness

Container plants are particularly prone to winter damage. Roots are less cold hardy than are the tops of plants. Container plants can have root damage at 15° F while the tops of the plant may still be alive. Use species that are hardy to at least one zone (10° F) colder than your area (see the Climate Zone Map on page 108), or affix movable bases to the containers so they can be moved to a protected location during the winter.

Maintaining Shrubs in Containers

Growing shrubs in containers is similar to growing plants in the ground (see pages 24 to 27), except that a few of the requirements are more critical.

Soil requirements   The soil used to fill containers is important. If the number or size of containers is not too large, consider using a lightweight, packaged soil mix. Proper drainage is vital with container-grown plants, and these mixes provide nearly perfect drainage.

When using soil from the garden to fill containers, mix in soil amendments, such as compost, peat moss, nitrogen-stabilized sawdust, leaf mold, ground fir bark, or pine bark. Add perlite to lighten the mix and improve drainage. At least half of the final mix should be made up of amendments; common proportions are 1 part garden soil, 1 part perlite or sand, and 1 part organic material.

When filling a container with soil, leave 2 or 3 inches between the top of the soil and the top of the pot. This space holds the water while it soaks through the soil to the bottom of the container, saving time and effort in watering.

Watering and feeding   Any plant in a container depends almost totally on the gardener for the water and nutrients necessary for growth. Unlike plants in the ground, the roots of a container shrub are very restricted. Therefore, water must be applied on a regular basis—as often as required to keep the foliage from wilting. To make sure that the soil is evenly wet throughout the container, apply water until it runs out the drainage hole.

Watering flushes nutrients through the container's soil much more rapidly than with plants growing in the ground. Compensate by lightly feeding plants in containers with a complete fertilizer as frequently as every two weeks during the active growing season of spring and summer, or use a slow-release fertilizer. Many gardeners prefer to feed container plants with liquid fertilizer because it is easy to apply. See page 35 for information about fertilizers.

New water-absorbent materials have been developed which can double the water retention capacity of potting soil. These super-absorbents are particularly useful in containers, and as little as a teaspoonful in a large pot will have significant results. Consult your local nursery or garden center for advice on selecting and using these materials.

Root care   Over a period of years, roots may fill a container and the shrub may become root-bound. When this condition occurs, either transplant the plant into a larger container or shave off part of the roots and add new soil to the container. When shaving roots, compensate for the root loss by lightly pruning the top of the plant. This process of revitalization should be repeated every few years or when, despite regular waterings and feedings, the shrub seems to have diminished in vigor.

Moving container plants   When moving container shrubs from one location to another, do it gradually. A radical change in environment can injure plants if made too abruptly. Be especially careful about moving a plant from the shade to a sunnier location; leaves used to the shade can be rapidly burned by the hot sun. Likewise, a plant acclimated to a sunny location produces unusually long branches and large leaves when moved suddenly to a shady spot. Change the location in a succession of small moves, allowing the shrub several days to adjust to each stage.

Many flowering shrubs can be moved inside the house for a few days of special attention during the blooming period. However, with any outdoor shrub, a stay indoors of more than five days is not recommended. While outdoor shrubs are inside, they should be kept in as cool a location as possible and especially kept away from direct exposure to dry furnace heat.

The Basics of Care

Shrubs are among the easiest of plants to care for. The right fertilizer at the right time, effective watering, protection from adverse weather, and solving common problems as they arise will help shrubs thrive.

One of the primary advantages of most shrubs is that, once established, they require little maintenance. Once a shrub has become accustomed to a location, its roots spread out through many cubic feet of soil, often far beyond the limits of the branches and deep into the ground. The large volume of soil reached by their roots provides shrubs with a wide source of water and nutrients and reduces their need for regular maintenance. Slow-growing shrubs are particularly independent of fertilizers; camellias, for example, often need no fertilizer as they do well on the nutrients released by decomposing mulch.

However, proper maintenance is important for most shrubs and will result in beautiful plants year after year. Basic maintenance considerations to keep in mind include watering thoroughly, using mulch to keep roots and soil healthy and to help retain moisture around root zones, adding nutrients at the right times for better blooms and foliage, protecting shrubs from severe weather, and inspecting shrubs closely to discover and control pests or diseases in their early stages.

The only other maintenance requirement is occasional pruning—the next chapter is devoted to this aspect of shrub gardening. This chapter provides guidance in watering, fertilizing, and protecting shrubs, as well as recognizing and solving common shrub problems. If you give your shrubs the care outlined in these pages, they will continue the healthy growth they started when you planted them.

The distinct design and vigorous health of the shrubs in this formal garden require regular care to maintain.

WATER

A shrub that has been chosen to suit its site demands special watering care only during the first few months after planting. During this period of initial establishment, a shrub's roots grow only about an inch into dry soil. Roots do not reach out in search of water; in fact, it is possible for a plant to die of thirst even when water is available just inches from the root tips. For a shrub to develop a healthy, extensive root system, the area in which the roots are to grow must be kept moist.

If the newly planted shrub is not served by an irrigation system, the most efficient way to ensure that it gets sufficient water is to create a watering basin (see page 27). At each watering, fill the basin twice, allowing the water to drain into the soil each time. If you have a number of shrubs to water, fill each basin, then repeat the process at the beginning again. An alternative is to water each shrub very slowly by putting the hose in the basin and turning the water on to a trickle. Set a kitchen timer for the length of time necessary to wet the soil thoroughly.

New shrubs become established in about six weeks, but they should be watched carefully for the first year. Make sure they receive sufficient amounts of water during that crucial first summer.

After Shrubs Are Established

Except in arid parts of the country, established shrubs seldom need to be watered. During periods of prolonged drought, water infrequently but thoroughly. Most native plants require no additional water and, in fact, are damaged by too much water. The reason established shrubs need little or no water from the ground surface is that their root systems are extensive. As a shrub's roots grow, they penetrate farther into the soil and draw on deeper reservoirs of moisture.

When you do water, remember to water slowly over a long period of time to allow the water to soak deep into the soil. Avoid frequent light watering as this leads to a shallow root system.

Testing for Soil Moisture

To check soil moisture, cut into the area around the shrub with a shovel or trowel to a depth of at least 4 inches, or use a soil moisture tester. Because the surrounding soil can be wet when the rootball is not, be sure the rootball itself is moist. Check by poking a finger into the rootball area. Do this every day until you know how much watering your new shrubs need to maintain the proper moisture level. For established plantings, make sure the deeper levels of soil contain enough moisture.

Test soil moisture at—and below—the ground surface.

Watering Problems

Most water problems are soil problems. For example, clay soils absorb and drain water very slowly. Air in the soil, necessary for healthy root growth, is minimal in clay soils, especially after watering. If water fills too many of the air spaces for too long, roots may die, causing top growth to die. Sandy soils, on the other hand, allow water to drain through rapidly, leaving plenty of air but little water. The middle range of loam soils have good water retention and drainage. See page 18 for a discussion of soil and soil treatments.

Irrigation Systems

Shrubs in the ground do not require regular watering, but if you install an irrigation system for your other plants and trees, consider including watering devices for your shrubs. Many kinds of systems are available, from conventional sprinklers to the more sophisticated drip systems (see below). Choose a system that suits the terrain and plants of your garden; any irrigation system will save work.

Keep shrub irrigation systems separate from those for lawns and other plants that require water more often. If the two systems are hooked together, the shrubs receive water too frequently and suffer as a result. Consult your local nursery or garden center for information on the types of sprinkler heads best suited for shrubs. Even with an automated sprinkler system, infrequent deep irrigation is better than frequent light watering.

Drip irrigation   Drip irrigation is a watering system of small plastic irrigation tubes installed directly next to each plant to be watered. Emitters (watering heads) located at appropriate points along the tubes deliver water to the plants slowly, a drop at a time. The water needs of the plant are supplied on an almost constant basis; the flow rate, which is fixed, ranges in volume from ½ to 2 gallons per hour.

Drip irrigation differs significantly from conventional watering methods, which provide much larger amounts of water at periodic intervals. Drip irrigation systems can be substantially less expensive than conventional sprinkler systems. They are simpler to install because they do not require calculation of water pressure. In addition, drip systems encourage deeper

rooting of plants than conventional watering systems as they water slowly and deeply in a controlled area. Drip systems are especially useful in areas of heavy soil.

Drip systems can be customized with the addition of a variety of equipment. Some of the most popular extras are fertilizer injectors, time clocks, and moisture sensors. Check at your local nursery or garden center for details on specific drip systems and accessories.

FERTILIZE

Most soils contain the nutrients shrubs need. However, fertilizers are sometimes needed to supplement this natural reservoir of nutrients and to make up for deficiencies. Experienced neighbors, nursery staff, or your county extension agent can tell you which nutrients are generally needed in your area. One nutrient, nitrogen, is needed in almost all areas, and is usually added routinely.

Shrubs demand little fertilizer compared to the amount required by lawns or vegetables. Light applications of fertilizer at regular intervals greatly increase growth and stimulate flower production.

Nutrients

Among other substances, commercial fertilizers contain three primary nutrients: nitrogen, phosphate, and potash (potassium); these are referred to by the acronym NPK. Fertilizers are labeled by percentages of these three nutrients. The percentages differ, but this order is always the same. The percentage variations reveal two important things. First, they tell how much of a nutrient is in the fertilizer by weight. In a 5-pound box of 5-10-10 fertilizer, 5 percent of that 5 pounds is nitrogen, 10 percent is phosphate, and 10 percent is potash. Furthermore, 5 pounds of 5-10-10 fertilizer contains only half as much nitrogen as 5 pounds of 10-12-16.

Second, the numbers tell the relative proportions of the three major nutrients. Ratios of 2-1-1 (like 10-5-5 or 20-10-10) indicate that there is twice as much nitrogen as phosphate and potash, and 1-2-2 ratios (like 5-10-10) indicate the opposite.

Although plants need all of these nutrients, each nutrient tends to stimulate different types of growth. Plants respond to different fertilizers according to the proportionate amounts of nutrients in them. Nitrogen tends to stimulate leafy growth, and phosphate and potash tend to further flowering, fruiting, and other kinds of growth. Ratios of 2-1-1 are normally used to promote leafing when plants are growing actively. Ratios of 1-1-1 or 1-2-2 are best used when plants are forming flower buds or growing new roots (in late summer).

When to Fertilize

Shrubs need nitrogen the most during periods of growth. For this reason, the heaviest application should be made just before or during rapid spring growth. In areas where the ground freezes in winter, nitrogen is sometimes also applied in the fall after top growth has stopped. Root growth, which continues into the winter and resumes in early spring, is stimulated by this practice. Heavy applications of nitrogen should not be made in late summer, or else new growth may start that does not have time to harden off by winter.

Because nitrogen stimulates leaf growth, it should be used in moderation on any shrub that you must prune regularly. Extra nitrogen on a hedge only means more frequent shearing for you.

If you want to promote flower or fruit production on shrubs that bloom in early spring, fertilize before the buds set in late summer. The fertilizer should have a low proportion of nitrogen (such as the 1-1-1 or 1-2-2 ratios), as too much nitrogen can keep some shrubs from setting flower buds and making fruit by diverting energy to leaf production.

Shrubs need phosphate and potash all the time they are growing, but these nutrients persist in the soil for long periods, so timing their application is only important if you specifically want to stimulate flowers or fruit.

MULCH

Any of the organic materials used as soil amendments can also be used as a mulch. The difference is in the way they are applied to the soil. A mulch is intended to remain on the surface of the soil—usually in a layer about 3 inches thick—whereas a soil amendment is incorporated into the soil.

A layer of mulch covering the root zone of a shrub helps keep the soil temperature cooler, thereby promoting root growth; keeps the soil moisture at a more even level, thus reducing the amount of watering needed; keeps weeds from germinating; and aids in the long-term development of good soil structure.

An organic mulch is most effective when it is renewed once or twice a year and is especially important around newly planted shrubs. Because organic matter floats in water, the best time to add it is after breaking down the water basin, usually about six weeks after planting (see page 27). Spread the mulch evenly around the root zone of the shrub, keeping it a couple of inches away from the stem of the plant. Moist mulch against the stem

Yellow leaves may be a sign of nitrogen deficiency.

encourages crown rot, the growth of various fungi, the breeding of insects, and the burrowing of mice and other rodents.

Any organic material can serve as a mulch, but certain kinds do better than others; finely ground fir or pine bark, pine straw, compost, well-rotted manure, and redwood soil conditioner are best. Peat moss makes a poor mulch because it forms a crust on top and becomes difficult to water. Check with your nursery or garden center for good mulching material that is readily available in your area.

CLIMATE PROTECTION

If shrubs are climatically adapted to the area in which they are planted, they rarely need protection from weather extremes. Only the occasional cold snap or heat spell demands protective measures for sensitive plants. However, when shrubs are grown outside their natural boundaries—for example, a frost-tender plant in the northern states or a shade-loving plant in direct sun—the microclimate surrounding these plants needs to be modified. Wind, heat, and cold are the most likely sources of plant damage.

Wind

One of the best means of protection from strong winds is a windbreak (see pages 14 and 15). A living windbreak can make the climate of your garden more enjoyable for both people and plants. Strong, hot winds accelerate water evaporation and transpiration. Plants that have not yet established extensive root systems can be easily toppled.

Heat

During periods of unusual heat, the most important protection you can give your shrubs is to keep them well watered. Do not let the soil around the plants dry out. Add mulch to keep the soil cool and moist. For plants that have especially tender foliage, build a simple, temporary structure to provide shade (see illustration at right). Sprinkling the leaves with water helps as emergency relief for larger shrubs. Although there are a few plants whose foliage might be damaged by such action, the benefits of a quick sprinkling during a hot spell far outweigh the drawbacks.

The best way to protect shrubs from excessive heat is to plant them suitably in the first place. For example, most shade-loving shrubs tolerate morning sun until about 11 a.m. and afternoon sun during the winter, but won't thrive in a location where they receive afternoon sun in the summer, especially if the heat reflects off of a wall or where searing winds are prevalent.

Cold

If you garden in an area where occasional hard frosts damage sensitive plants, pay attention to the weather reports. Knowing in advance that early morning temperatures are going to be unusually low allows you to take protective measures the night before. If the shrubs are in movable containers, bring them close to the house where they receive protection from the eaves. If the shrubs are stationary, cover them with burlap, cardboard, or

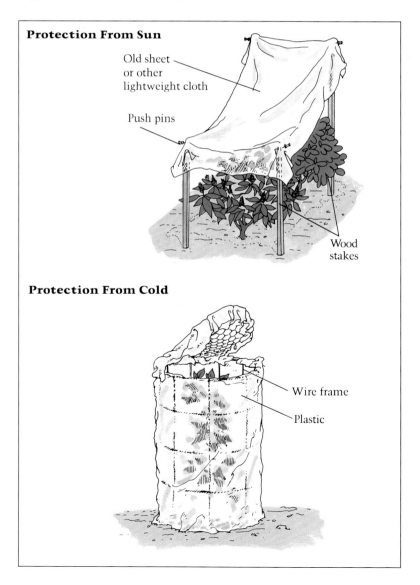

Protection From Sun

Old sheet or other lightweight cloth

Push pins

Wood stakes

Protection From Cold

Wire frame

Plastic

plastic. Be sure to remove this protection the following morning.

To protect tender plants in an area that has regular frosts, build a lightweight structure that can be used from year to year. Cover the structure tightly with fabric or plastic so that warm air rising from the ground and the plant is trapped during the night.

Tender deciduous shrubs grown in areas of extreme cold require special protection to make it through the winter. A coarse mulch, such as leaves or straw, should be packed around the crown of a plant or around, if necessary, the entire plant. Hold the mulch in place with a wire cylinder.

Winter damage to broad-leafed evergreens is frequently the result of leaf transpiration, which continues when the soil is solidly frozen so that water is unavailable to the plants.

To prevent this kind of damage, water thoroughly if the soil is dry—water holds heat, and a moist soil freezes more slowly than a dry soil. Mulch the shrub heavily to provide insulation to the soil surrounding roots. Spray an antitranspirant, available at garden centers and nurseries, on the leaves to retard drying. This also helps coniferous shrubs. Because snow can damage shrubs—particularly needled evergreens—by packing on the branches and breaking or flattening them from the accumulated weight, tie the boughs of the plant with cord before the first snow.

SOLVING COMMON SHRUB PROBLEMS

The key to solving plant problems easily is to recognize symptoms as soon as they occur and then act promptly to treat problems while they are still minor.

Detecting Problems

Familiarity with shrubs in the garden can help you detect problems early and allow for quick treatment. A daily stroll, with an eye for problems as well as beauty, is the most pleasant and least time-consuming way to keep in touch with the garden.

What do you look for? Anything that looks irregular: a chewed leaf, compacted soil, stunted foliage, a branch that is growing too far in the wrong direction. If you are familiar with your plants, you will be quick to see obvious clues, but you'll also be able to avoid trouble before problems happen.

You know things about your own garden that no book can tell you. Colors, textures, and vigor are all indicators of overall plant health, and only you know what's normal for your garden and what's not. Get into the garden as often as possible—you'll notice subtle but important changes that signal the current health conditions of your plants.

Avoiding Problems

A vigorously growing shrub is less susceptible to injury from insects and diseases than one that is under stress from lack of water or nutrients. Bark beetles, borers, and sucking insects do more damage during or after a drought than at any other time.

Besides having to put up with insects and diseases, plants sometimes suffer from actions

---

Precautions When Using Chemicals

Many pesticides, fungicides, and herbicides are available for the control of pests, diseases, and weeds. The two most important steps in pest and disease control are proper identification of the pest or disease and correct application of the product. Whenever you use a chemical spray, be sure to follow the steps outlined below.

Mixing

For your safety and for best results, read and be sure you understand the entire label before using any garden chemical, and follow the directions faithfully.

When mixing these chemicals, always work on a clean, firm surface near a water source. Measure all products carefully to ensure their proper dilution. Never make up more of a solution than you need at one time.

Do not eat or smoke while mixing or spraying, and wash your hands thoroughly when you're done.

Spraying

With pesticides, application is key. Be sure to spray the pests and their hiding places adequately, as the label directs. Never spray any plant that is suffering from a lack of moisture. Water deeply and thoroughly a day before spraying.

Avoid spraying altogether if the air temperature is above 85° F or if it is exceptionally windy. In hot weather, some chemical formulations may burn the foliage. When it is windy, the spray can drift to areas where it is not wanted.

The label will instruct you either to spray just enough to wet the foliage or to spray to the drip point, where the leaf surfaces are holding all the spray they can, and any more will drip off. In either case, be sure to spray all plant surfaces thoroughly. Don't forget the bottoms of leaves and both sides of stems and twigs.

Cleaning Up

Thoroughly rinse the sprayer before putting it back on the shelf. Also, rinse out empty chemical containers that you intend to dispose of—never burn empty containers. Allow the sprayer to drain upside down for 30 seconds. Then rinse thoroughly with water and allow to dry before storing.

taken by the gardener; careless skinning of a shrub's bark with a lawn mower, for example, could allow entrance to borers or fungi. Here are some simple steps that will help prevent problems in your garden.

☐ Keep old leaves picked up—they are often the source of infection for various diseases and a safe hiding place for many damaging insects. Composted leaves, however, pose no problem.

☐ Keep pruning shears sharp, and use them correctly. Bark tears easily and heals slowly. Many insects and diseases will attack only if there is an opening in the bark.

☐ Pull weeds early, before they offer competition to surrounding plants and bear seeds. The best time to pull them is when the ground is soft from rain or watering.

☐ Spray at the first sign of disease or insect attack. Quick action results in more complete treatment, and less damage to plants.

☐ Remove and destroy—by burning or throwing away—any diseased flowers or fruits. Disease spores can live on them from one season to the next.

☐ Practice a thorough cleanup before winter sets in. Remove debris and other likely homes for overwintering insects and diseases.

☐ To promote healthier plants and to keep the weed population to a minimum, keep a 3-inch layer of mulch on all open areas of ground. Cover the root zones of shrubs, as well, but keep the mulch a few inches away from stems or trunks. See page 36 on mulching.

Sources for Information

Local problems in the control of pests and diseases are under constant study by the research departments of your state university. You can obtain publications on the results of their studies at the office of your county extension agent. Many are available free, others at a nominal cost. County extension agents are listed in the local telephone book under county government offices. A telephone call will bring you a list of available publications. Or you can write the state extension office for a list of publications and the addresses of the county agents.

Local or regional arboretums and botanic gardens can be valuable resources as well. Check the yellow pages of your telephone book. *The Ortho Problem Solver*, available at many garden centers, is another resource for information on shrub problems and solutions.

Take proper precautions when applying any plant sprays: Wear protective gloves and point the nozzle away from you.

Regular care has kept this old boxwood hedge and topiary healthy.

Pruning

Pruning is essential to the maintenance of most garden shrubs. It is also a way to shape shrubs to meet the design needs of the garden. Proper pruning requires knowing basic pruning techniques— how and when to apply the cuts—and understanding how a shrub will grow in response to various types of pruning cuts.

P runing can be used to direct the growth of shrubs, to improve their health, and to increase their production of flowers and fruit. Pruning can direct a shrub's growth to balance unevenness, keep a shrub small and compact, make it grow tall, or open up its form. Using different cuts, shrubs may be shaped to achieve a formal or natural look, make a hedge, or create a topiary sculpture.

The basics of pruning are simple: what and how to prune and when to do it. This chapter provides the basics of good pruning care for shrubs and includes guidelines for pruning to control and direct shrub form. In addition there is information on renewing old shrubs and establishing regular pruning cycles to keep shrubs thriving for years to come. Special pruning techniques for roses, rhododendrons, and azaleas are included. For more detailed information on pruning all types of plants, refer to Ortho's book *All About Pruning*.

Periodic shearing is important for both the health and appearance of hedges.

PRUNING STYLES

There are two basic styles of pruning: the natural style, which responds to the natural pattern of a shrub's growth, and the formal style, which includes espaliers, topiaries, hedges, and other severely shaped specimens.

Natural

The natural look is achieved by working with the shrub's natural growth habit. Refer to the "Plant Selection Guide" beginning on page 51; the naturally occurring form is included in each shrub description. The type of pruning that results in a natural shape is called thinning (see page 43).

Formal

A formal effect is possible either through careful and consistent pruning or by planting varieties of shrubs that are naturally neat and compact. If the shrubs in your garden are not naturally inclined to compactness, occasional heading back (see page 43) or frequent shearing is necessary to create a tailored, formal look. Shear plants frequently, taking off a small amount of growth each time so that the plants maintain a consistent appearance.

WHEN TO PRUNE

Shrubs require pruning at different times of the year. Shrubs that are grown primarily for their flowers require greater attention to timing than coniferous and broad-leafed evergreen shrubs. Flowering shrubs are divided into two groups: those that flower on old wood and those that flower on new wood. On this basis alone, you can determine when to prune your flowering shrubs.

To determine whether a shrub blooms on new or old wood, first distinguish between the two types of growth. New wood is new stem growth that is produced during the current growing season. It is usually light green or pinkish in color. Old wood has grown during a previous season. It is usually much darker in color than new wood and is much more brittle. While a plant blooms, take a close look to see where the flowers form. If you are uncertain about whether the shrub blooms on old or new wood, wait a season to discover whether it blooms or not, and if it does, on what type of wood.

Once you know the type of wood on which a shrub flowers, pruning is easy. In early spring,

Top: The naturally beautiful shape of this laceleaf Japanese maple (Acer palmatum var. dissectum) has been enhanced by careful pruning. Bottom: Clipping foliage results in tight, dense shapes.

old-wood-blooming shrubs should be pruned a week or two after the flowers drop. Pruning during the dormant season would remove the blossom buds. When pruned at the right time—in the spring or early summer—the plants have the rest of the season to produce more blossom buds for the following year.

Shrubs that blossom in late spring or in the summer produce flowers on new wood. The time to prune these shrubs is during the dormant season, or just before growth starts in very early spring. Pruning at these times encourages more new stem growth and more blossoms.

TYPES OF PRUNING

The two basic pruning methods are thinning and heading. Thinning, or thinning out, removes entire branches back to a main trunk, or major branches to the ground. Heading, or heading back, removes only part of a branch.

The main difference between thinning and heading is the effect on plants. Thinning causes the shrub's energy to go to the remaining branches which then grow more. The long-term result of thinning a shrub is to give it an open, natural look. Thinned shrubs become larger than shrubs that are headed back.

Heading back a branch causes the plant to grow multiple branches in place of a single branch. Heading forces the dormant buds closest to a pruning cut to grow. Over the long term, heading results in a more dense shrub that has more branches, but is smaller than a shrub that has been thinned. Heading is most often associated with formal shapes.

Two special forms of heading are called pinching and shearing. They have the same effect as other heading cuts, but are accomplished in different ways. Pinching is done with the fingertips. A pinch removes only the growing point of a branch, allowing the lateral buds near the end of the branch to grow. This usually results in two, three, or four growing points where there had been only one. Pinching is used to make a small plant bushy and thick or to redirect energy within the plant, guiding its growth as it develops.

Shearing, or clipping, also removes only the growing points. The difference is that unlike pinching, shearing—accomplished with hedge shears or power trimmers—removes most of a shrub's growing points. The effect is the same: the plant responds by increasing the number of its growing points. Shearing is used to make hedges or topiary and is associated with formal styles.

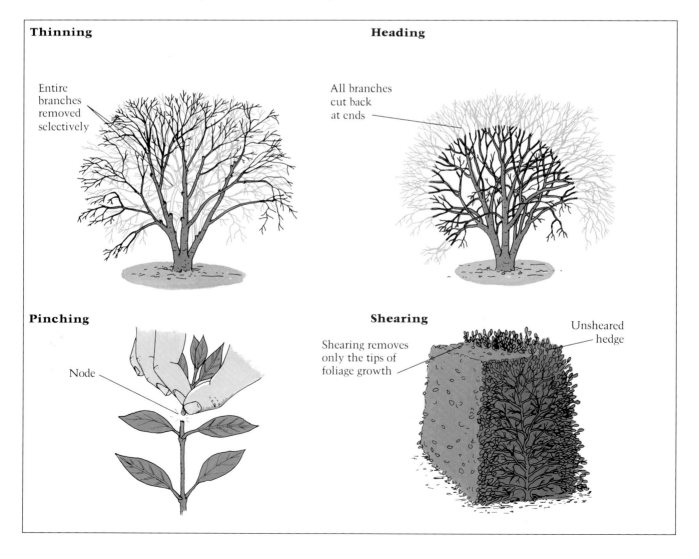

Thinning

Entire branches removed selectively

Heading

All branches cut back at ends

Pinching

Node

Shearing

Shearing removes only the tips of foliage growth

Unsheared hedge

Pruning Cuts

Before leaves and new stems appear, growth buds form in small swellings on the stems and branches of a shrub. Inside these buds are tiny, undeveloped leaves, branches, and flowers. There are two types of buds: terminal and lateral (see illustration below). Terminal buds grow at the tip of a shoot, and lateral buds appear at the side. These buds are the keys to making good pruning cuts. When pruning,

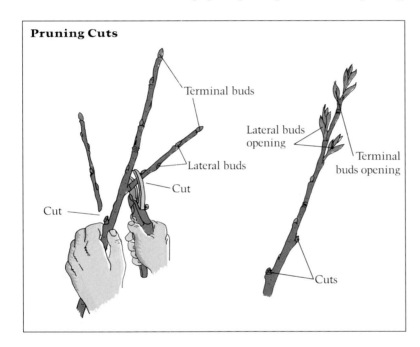

Pruning Cuts

Terminal buds

Lateral buds opening

Lateral buds

Terminal buds opening

Cut

Cut

Cuts

Topiary is the most extreme and recognizable characteristic of formal gardens and requires regular shearing.

always cut above a bud. To place the cut near a lateral bud, select a bud that is pointing outward so that the new branch will grow away from the main trunk rather than crisscrossing with interior branches. Cutting above an outward-pointing lateral bud will also open up the plant to light and air and promote orderly growth—important goals in pruning.

Cutting off lateral buds or side branches will direct the shrub's energy to the terminal buds, thus pushing the branches to grow in the directions they are already pointing. When making a pruning cut, hold the branch just below where the cut will be. Place the cutting blade of the hand pruners beneath the branch and cut at an upward angle. The slant of the cut should be in the direction you want the new branch to grow. Never leave a budless stub of wood behind. Stubs are unsightly and usually die and become an entry point for insects and diseases. Consider each cut carefully—no pruning cut should ever be made without a good reason and a clear understanding of what the results are likely to be.

Topiary

Shrubs shaped into geometrical, animal, and other forms to create living garden sculptures are called topiaries. The ideal choice for a topiary plant is a finely textured and hardy evergreen. The two varieties most often used are boxwood (*Buxus*) and yew (*Taxus*). Creating topiary requires a great deal of patience. For example, to develop a simple double-balled shape can take 5 years for boxwood and 10 years for yew. To create a more complex animal form may require twice that long.

The easiest topiary to shape is the double ball. Start with a young, 1-gallon plant with plenty of low branches that will fill out close to the ground. After pruning the lower portion into a ball shape, select several strong branches and let them grow at least 2 feet above the first ball. Then strip the foliage off the bottom foot to form the separating stem and begin to shape the top foot of growth into the second ball.

Espaliers

Shrubs or trees that are trained to grow flat against a vertical plane are called espaliers. Almost any shrub with fairly limber growth can be espaliered. All shrubs should have 6 inches between themselves and the wall or fence. Wire or wooden supports fixed at that distance will allow both for air movement and room for the branches to develop.

Start with a shrub that has a strong central stem. After planting the shrub, run the wires (or supports) horizontally at intervals of 18 inches across the wall or fence. Then cut off the central stem at 18 inches, just below the height of the first wire. This activates shoots to appear just below the cut.

During the first growing season, allow only three new shoots to develop. Train two shoots horizontally onto the wire, and let the other one grow vertically as an extension of the central trunk. Rub off all the growth from the lower trunk.

As the plant grows, cut off the new trunk a little below the second 36-inch-high wire. This activates a second set of shoots. Train these as you did the first set. Continue training the shrub in this manner until all the wires are covered with branches. When you have formed the basic espalier frame you want, keep new growth restricted with frequent pinching during the summer.

Hedges

Hedge plants should be pruned when they are first set out. Bare-root plants, intended to produce a dense hedge, should be pruned to about half of their original height. Plants from containers, and other plants that naturally produce an open hedge, should be pruned back by about one third on both the tops and the sides.

Let a newly planted hedgerow grow without shearing for a full growing season to give the roots a chance to become established. The second year, trim the hedge lightly to keep it dense as it grows. Don't try to achieve too quickly the hedge height you want. Continue shearing lightly to keep the hedge thick, without gaps, as it grows to the desired height. Once the hedge is as tall as you want it, your pruning technique should change.

Shear small-leafed hedges, such as boxwood or yew, whenever they look ragged from uneven new growth, and take off almost all the new growth. Let the hedge retain a little bit of new growth each time you shear by cutting about ¼ inch farther out than you cut at the last shearing. This will avoid leaving bare spots and clusters of cut branches. Allowing

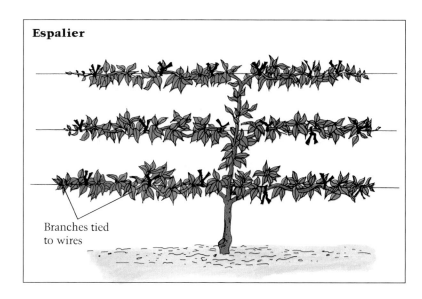

Espalier

Branches tied to wires

this slow growth ensures that the hedge will always have a fresh new layer of leaves. When, after 10 or 15 years of this slow growth, the hedge becomes too large, cut it back severely early one spring and let it begin its slow growth cycle again.

Shearing a large-leafed hedge cuts many leaves in half, giving the hedge a butchered look. It is better to prune these hedges one branch at a time with a pair of hand shears. Make the cuts inside the layer of foliage so that they are hidden, leaving only fresh, uncut leaves on the surface.

To keep a hedge leafed out down to the ground, shape it so that the top is narrower than the bottom, letting light to the whole side of the hedge. Leaves that do not get enough light drop off. Shaping a hedge in this way is especially important on the northern side, or on any part of the hedge that is in the shade.

Solving Hedge Problems

Hedges that have been allowed to go their own way for a number of seasons develop several common problems. Often they have grown too tall and spindly, have bare spots, or lean into a neighbor's yard. All of these problems can be taken care of with corrective pruning.

Hedges that have grown too tall and floppy have usually been allowed to grow too fast. Hedges should be developed carefully. Regular pruning encourages a sturdy structure and strengthens a mass of wispy stems. If the structure of the hedge is very weak, it can be cut back to the ground and allowed to grow up again at a more controlled rate.

Top: This pruned hedge forms a neat enclosure for pieris shrubs.
Bottom: Prune large-leafed hedges with hand shears, hiding the cuts inside the layer of foliage.

Hedges develop bare, leafless undersides—often referred to as barebottom—from lack of sunlight at the bottom of the hedge. The problem may also be aggravated by a lack of water and nutrients. Cut the hedge back heavily to stimulate new growth at the bottom, then shape it properly as it grows. Water regularly and provide enough fertilizer for vigorous growth.

A hedge that leans into the neighbor's yard is often caused by only one side of the hedge—yours—being trimmed. One solution is to reduce the height and width of the hedge dramatically, letting it grow back with an even, strong structure. The three- or five-year system of renewal also works well in this case (see page 47). If necessary, offer to prune your neighbor's side when you prune your own to keep the hedge balanced.

Bare spots in a hedge are caused by old age and repeated shearings without allowing the hedge to grow. The problem can be alleviated by cutting away the dead twigs branch by branch and then, in the future, by shearing ¼ inch outside the last cut.

REVITALIZING OLD SHRUBS

Old, neglected shrubs often require extensive pruning to make them attractive parts of the garden landscape again. Start revitalizing an older shrub by clearing away weak, thin shoots. This opens up the plant, allowing sunshine to reach its center while retaining the older branches, which usually have considerable character. Cut away branches that point inward or that cross other branches.

Next, study the plant's new form. Does it make an interesting silhouette, or does it still need errant branches trimmed away? Before cutting off any major branches, have someone pull the branch back as far as it will go without breaking it. What does the shrub look like without it? Does the shrub need additional thinning out to make it less massive, or does it need trimming around the edges to give it a more compact, neat look?

Many older shrubs act like small trees, growing to heights never mentioned in catalogs and gardening books. Mature specimens can be the focal point of an entire landscape, especially if the foliage and branches that conceal the trunk are trimmed away. Follow-up thinning the next year can help revitalize an old specimen. Growth taken away at the base of an old shrub can be concealed by planting new shrubs beneath it—or you may find the additional space desirable, particularly in a small garden.

If the top part of a shrub is unattractive, cut the shrub completely to the ground. As long as the plant has the strength to push out new shoots and leaves, it will have enough strength to replace what was cut off. By cutting off the shrub as close to the ground as possible, new growth will be generated from the roots rather than from older branches. The best time to prune severely is late winter or early spring. Treat the resulting new growth like that of a new shrub.

Some shrubs can be killed by cutting them back too far. If you are uncertain how a shrub will respond to a radical pruning, head one branch back to a leafless stub to see how it responds. If the stub sprouts new growth, the shrub can probably safely be cut back.

RENEWAL PRUNING

Renewal pruning is a special form of pruning that can keep deciduous shrubs, particularly flowering varieties, young and vital no matter how old they are. Even though the plant itself may be over one hundred years old, this technique produces branches that never get more than three to five years old.

Every year or two, prune out a few of the oldest canes at ground level. Removing this old wood opens up the top to let light and air into the interior of the shrub and encourages growth from the base, eventually renewing the top of the plant.

For those shrubs that do not produce shoots from their base, such as viburnums and euonymus, deadheading the plant—removing the dead blooms—allows the vegetative buds of the plant to grow. In most of the United States, there are one to two periods of vegetative growth, followed by flower bud development in late July and August.

Three-Year Renewal

Each year, most deciduous shrubs produce shoots from their base or roots. Prune the shrub so that one third of the shoots will be one year old, one third will be two years old, and one third will be three years old. When you prune, remove crossing limbs or any dead

The bottom of this pittosporum hedge has become bare from being shaded by the wider top.

or diseased branches. Next, cut out most of the three-year-old wood. This will induce new shoots to spring up, leaving the desired number to form the first-year shoots the following year.

The only other pruning necessary is done to reduce the total height of the shrub to keep it within the bounds you desire, while preserving its natural form. Removing the third-year wood every year after blooming guarantees that you always have young, healthy wood to produce the biggest and healthiest flowers. The three-year renewal system also results in healthier plants because older wood is more susceptible to insects and disease than young, strong shoots.

Five-Year Renewal

This approach is the same as the three-year system, except that the process is spread over five years. Slow-growing shrubs respond well to two additional years of thinning. Adjust to allow for the fact that there are not as many new shoots each year with this method as with the three-year system.

Flowering shrubs that have a moundlike habit of growth, such as summer-flowering spireas and florist's hydrangea should be pruned yearly by thinning out some of the weakest canes and cutting the rest back to varying heights so that the flowers will not all bloom at the same level.

SHRUBS FOR SPECIAL TREATMENT

A few shrubs need special treatment to stay healthy and attractive. Rhododendrons, azaleas, and roses are three common ones.

Rhododendrons and Azaleas

The hundreds of kinds of rhododendrons and azaleas require more grooming than pruning. The spent flower heads of rhododendrons should be removed, a process called deadheading. Tips of azaleas should be pinched out to make the plants bushier. When removing the spent flowers and tips, care must be taken not to remove the next year's buds.

Fingertips are the most effective means for most of the pruning of this group of plants. Only older plants that have become leggy, sparse, or damaged may require a few cuts with hand pruners or loppers.

The difference between a rhododendron and an azalea lies in where the buds are placed, and this causes them to need different types of pruning. Because a rhododendron bud is always found just above the leaf rosette, cut

just above the bud. On an azalea, however, the bud is concealed under the bark along the entire branch, so cuts may be made anywhere along the branch without affecting flowering.

Rhododendrons These shrubs must have their spent flowers removed. If seedpods are left on the plant, they consume much of the energy that could go into flowers or leaves. Hold the branch with the faded flower in one hand, and with the other hand carefully snap off the flower head with a slight sideways pressure, taking care not to harm the growth buds below—these are next year's flowers and leaves. Injuring flower buds will prevent flower growth the next year. If your plant is too tall to handpick thoroughly, use a hose to wash dead petals away. If they are not deadheaded, rhododendrons tend to bloom only in alternate years.

Azaleas These require even less pruning than rhododendrons. They should be tip-pinched, particularly when young, to produce bushier plants. Do this within a couple of weeks after the plant blooms.

When azaleas become older, stronger pruning may become necessary. Because of the distribution of buds along the entire branch, an azalea can be cut anywhere. Azaleas may even be sheared. Although shearing destroys the natural shape of the plant, it produces a crop of flowers at the sheared surface.

To rejuvenate an older azalea that has grown too woody and leggy, prune it over a period of two or three years. The first year, cut back the oldest branches to within 10 to 12 inches of the ground. The next year, do the same thing, and repeat this the third year. Never cut off more than one third of the plant each year. In this way, you can safely transform the azalea into a compact, bushy plant that produces an astonishing crop of flowers.

Roses

The many members of the genus *Rosa* are a varied lot, but their growth patterns may be classified in two groups for pruning purposes: those that bloom all summer and those that only bloom for a couple of weeks in the spring. Prune spring-blooming roses when they finish blooming. Prune heavily to encourage new growth, which bears the next year's flowers.

The small buds beside this rhododendron flower are next year's flowers and leaves and must not be broken when removing spent blooms.

Prune roses that bloom all summer—hybrid teas, floribundas, and grandifloras—when they are dormant, usually in late spring just before they begin growth.

The first step in pruning roses is to remove all dead wood and weak twigs. Next, open up the center of the plant by pruning out canes that cross inward. Remove any canes that have gotten too old to produce well. These canes make branches that are weak and twiggy and that branch frequently. The branches are rough and dark with old bark and may show signs of decay.

Next, determine how vigorous the rose is. And, if the new canes are ¾ inch in diameter or more, the rose is vigorous. Slender canes indicate a weaker shrub. The general rule is, the less vigorous the rose, the harder you prune it. Pruning less vigorous roses removes growing points (dormant buds) that will use up energy when the shrub begins growing in the spring. The fewer buds you leave, the more energy each growing point will have.

Leave about six canes on the most vigorous roses. On the least vigorous, leave only three. Head back the canes by about one third of their length. Heading them back more makes fewer, but larger, flowers. A lighter pruning produces more, smaller flowers and a more attractive shrub shape. Prune heavily if you want to produce flowers for cutting, lightly if you want a more attractive garden shrub.

As the flowers are picked, cut the stem back to just above a leaf that has five leaflets. This leaf has a strong dormant bud at its base to make a good replacement cane.

If your rose bush gets too high by the end of the summer, or if the flowers are cut with long stems, cut each stem back so that only the two lowest five-leaflet leaves are left. This will slow the growth of the shrub.

Climbing roses have long canes that do not flower; flowers are produced on laterals. If the rose is on a trellis, untie the canes and lay them on the ground. Then, prune out all but the strongest three to five canes, and cut all the laterals back to two or three buds. Without cutting them shorter, tie the canes back up on their trellis, and arch them over at the top. This stops their upright growth and encourages laterals to form.

When picking roses, cut the stems just above a five-leaflet leaf. This leaf will have the strong bud to make the next flower.

Pruning a Shrub Rose

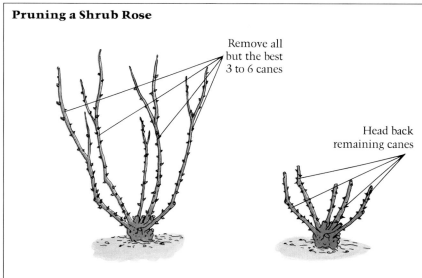

Remove all but the best 3 to 6 canes

Head back remaining canes

Pruning a Climbing Rose

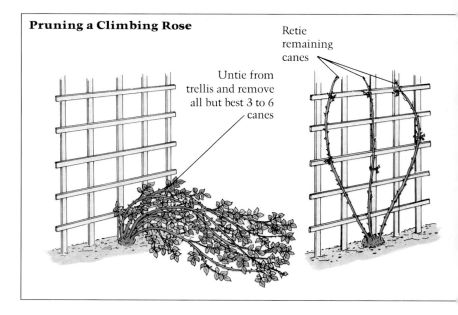

Untie from trellis and remove all but best 3 to 6 canes

Retie remaining canes

Plant Selection Guide

One of the most valuable tools for any gardener is a good plant list. This chapter includes lists of shrubs for specific uses, from dwarfs for small-space gardening to shrubs for special effects, followed by complete descriptions of each.

More than six thousand shrubs are raised commercially for sale, and new species, varieties, and cultivars are added every day. Shrubs of almost any flower and foliage color, cultural requirements, size, shape, and habit are available to the home gardener. Special varieties and cultivars have been developed to fill special needs. To help simplify this enormous selection, the following plant guide has been narrowed to a select, representative listing of approximately five hundred shrubs suited to a wide variety of design, horticultural, and special needs.

Plants are identified two ways: by common names and by botanical names. Common names, although in some cases easier to remember or to pronounce, have the disadvantage of not being consistent. One plant often has several common names, varying from region to region, even from person to person. And one common name may refer to entirely different plants in other countries or regions.

The *International Code of Nomenclature for Cultivated Plants* is the worldwide authority for horticultural names. The code ensures that every plant has a single botanical name. Botanical names are always Latin and are divided into two parts: genus and species. The

---

Varieties of silverberry (Elaeagnus pungens *'Aurea'*), *top; juniper* (Juniperus horizontalis), *center; and nandina* (Nandina domestica *'Nana purpurea'*), *bottom, display the remarkable beauty and range that exists among shrubs.*

genus is analogous to a surname, indicating a general group of plants. For example, *Acer* is the generic name for the maple tree. The species, which follows the generic name, is a more specific category within the genus. For example, *Acer palmatum* is a specific maple, the Japanese maple.

The variety is a further subdivision of a species. A variety is distinguished by the ability to pass on its identifying traits through its seed. It is usually discovered by accident or in the wild. Botanical varieties are indicated in Latin, follow the species name, and are preceded by the abbreviation *var.* For example, *Acer palmatum* var. *dissectum* is the laceleaf Japanese maple.

A cultivar, or cultivated variety, is similar to a variety, except that it passes on its particular traits either through seed or vegetative reproduction, such as cuttings or grafting, and is usually the product of deliberate horticultural development. Cultivars are set off by single quotation marks (or the abbreviation *cv.*), are rarely Latin, and they follow the name of either the species or the variety: for example, *Acer palmatum* var. *dissectum* 'Crimson King'. When discussing a generalized group of plants, often *variety* is used more generally to refer both to botanical varieties and to cultivars.

Each listing in the Plant Selection Guide includes the most frequently used common name or names. However, some plants—*Photinia* × *fraseri,* for example—have no common name.

Each plant entry in this chapter includes a range of hardiness zones—based upon the Climate Zone Map (see page 108)—indicating the northern and southern limits in which the plant can be grown. Find your zone on the map and use it as a reference when consulting this guide. However, as local conditions of temperature, rainfall, and other hardiness factors all vary within a region, this information should be used only as a starting point in selecting shrubs. Check with your local nursery to be sure the shrub will grow in your area.

In order to simplify the process of shrub selection, no more than a few cultivars for a particular plant are included. Many plants (junipers and other dwarf conifers, for example) offer a huge number of cultivars. Moreover, cultivars are best selected on a highly regional basis. This can best be done by calling upon the expertise and experience of your local nursery,

which is tailored to the exact requirements of your area.

Most of the shrubs included in this guide are popular enough to be offered by most nurseries in regions where they can be grown. A few, however, may be too new, too difficult to propagate, or too expensive to be widely available, and this is indicated in the description. In such cases, you may need to search a bit harder to find them. Your nursery may be able to special-order them for you, or you may be able to locate them through mail-order or specialty firms. Your local university, arboretum, or botanic garden may be further sources of assistance.

PLANT SELECTION LISTS

When you are searching for the right shrub for a particular problem or need, organized lists can be particularly helpful. Use the lists that follow to direct you to the appropriate description in the Gallery of Shrubs, later in this chapter. In some cases, species or cultivars are listed which do not appear in the Gallery of Shrubs; for further information on these, consult your local nursery.

Shrubs for Special Uses

The lists that follow include shrubs suited to special uses. See A Gallery of Shrubs (page 64) for complete descriptions.

Shrubs With Colorful Foliage the Year
    Around, p. 53
Shrubs for Winter Interest, p. 54
Shrubs That Tolerate Shade, p. 54
Shrubs for the Coldest Winters, p. 55
Drought-Tolerant Shrubs, p. 55
Shrubs for City Dwellers, p. 56
Shrubs With Fall Foliage Color, p. 56
Shrubs With Fragrant Flowers, p. 57
Fast-Growing Shrubs, p. 58
Shrubs That Attract Birds, p. 58
Shrubs for Containers, p. 58
Thorny Shrubs for Barriers, p. 59
Shrubs for Acid Soils, p. 59
Shrubs for Wet Soils, p. 60
Shrubs for Ground Covers, p. 60
Shrubs With Showy Fruit, p. 60
Shrubs That Are Easy to Care For, p. 61
Shrubs for Hedges and Other Formal
    Shapes, p. 61
Shrubs for the Seacoast, p. 62
Dwarf Shrubs, p. 62

Shrubs With Colorful Foliage The Year Around

Bright colors can be available in your garden all year long if you select shrubs for their colorful foliage. Deciduous plants are included in the list below, and evergreen varieties are marked with an asterisk (*). All should be placed with care, as brightly colored leaves make a bold statement in the landscape.

Acer palmatum var. *dissectum* laceleaf Japanese maple

Cultivars: 'Crimson King' (reddish), 'Flavescens' (yellowish green), 'Ozaka-zuki' (yellowish), 'Purpureum' (deep red), and 'Reticulatum' (green, yellow, and pink).

Aucuba japonica Japanese aucuba

Cultivars: *'Crotonifolia' (green and yellow), *'Picturata' (green and yellow), and *'Variegata' (green and yellow).

Berberis thunbergii Japanese barberry

Cultivars: 'Aurea' (yellow), 'Crimson Pygmy' (reddish), 'Sheridan's Red' (red), and 'Variegata' (white and green).

Chamaecyparis lawsoniana Lawson false-cypress

Cultivars: 'Forsteckensis' (gray-green) and *'Pygmaea Argentea' (yellow).

Chamaecyparis obtusa Hinoki false-cypress

Cultivar: *'Mariesii' (green tipped with white).

Chamaecyparis pisifera Sawara false-cypress

Cultivars: *'Aurea Nana' (yellow), *'Boulevard' (gray), *'Golden Mop' (yellow), and *'Nana Variegata' (green and white).

Cornus alba 'Argenteo-marginata' variegated Tartarian dogwood

Cultivar: 'Spaethii' (green and yellow).

Cotinus coggygria smoke tree

Cultivars: 'Daydream' (purple) and 'Velvet Cloak' (purple).

Smoke tree (Cotinus coggygria)

Daphne odora winter daphne

Cultivar: 'Marginata' (green and yellow).

Elaeagnus pungens silverberry

Cultivars: *'Maculata' (green and yellow), *'Marginata' (green and white), and *'Variegata' (green and yellow).

Euonymus fortunei winter-creeper, spindle tree

Cultivars: *'Emerald and Gold' (green and yellow), and *'Golden Prince' (green and yellow).

Euonymus japonica evergreen euonymus, Japanese spindle tree

Cultivars: *'Albomarginata' (green and white), *'Aureomarginata' (green and yellow), *'Golden' (green and yellow), *'Microphylla Variegata' (green and white), *'Silver King' (green and white), and *'Silver Queen' (green and white).

Hydrangea macrophylla bigleaf hydrangea, French hydrangea

Cultivar: 'Tricolor' (green, white, and yellow).

Juniperus chinensis Chinese juniper

Cultivars: *'Armstrongii' (gray), *'Blaauw' (gray), *'Old Gold' (yellow), *'Pfitserana Aurea' (yellow), and *'Plumosa Aureovariegata' (yellow).

Variety: *sargentii* (gray).

**Juniperus chinensis procumbens*
Japanese garden juniper (gray)

Juniperus communis common juniper

Cultivar: *'Depressa Aurea' (yellow).

**Juniperus conferta* shore juniper (gray-blue)

**Juniperus horizontalis* creeping juniper (gray or blue)

Juniperus sabina savin juniper

Cultivars: *'Broadmoor' (gray), *'Skandia' (gray), and *'Variegata' (gray and white).

Juniperus scopulorum Rocky Mountain juniper

Cultivars: *'Lakewood Globe' (gray-blue) and *'Table Top Blue' (blue-gray).

Kerria japonica Japanese rose

Cultivars: 'Aureo-variegata' (green and yellow), 'Aureo-vittata' (green and yellow stems), and 'Picta' (green and white).

Leptospermum scoparium New Zealand tea-tree

Cultivars: *'Gaiety Girl' (reddish) and *'Waringi' (reddish).

Leucothoe fontanesiana drooping leucothoe

Cultivar: *'Girard's Rainbow' (green, white, and pink).

Ligustrum × *ibolium* ibolium privet

Cultivar: 'Variegata' (green and yellow).

Ligustrum japonicum Japanese privet

Cultivar: *'Silver Star' (green and white).

Common winterberry (Ilex verticillata)

Japanese rose (Kerria japonica)

Ligustrum ovalifolium California privet
    Cultivar: *'Aureum' (green and yellow).

Ligustrum 'Vicaryi' golden privet (yellow)

Myrtus communis myrtle
    Cultivars: *'Compacta Variegata' (green and white) and 'Variegata' (green and white).

Nandina domestica nandina, heavenly-bamboo
    Cultivars: *'Nana Purpurea' (purplish) and 'Variegata' (green and white).

Osmanthus heterophyllus holly olive
    Cultivars: *'Purpureus' (purplish) and 'Variegatus' (green and white).

*****Photinia × fraseri** (red)

*****Pieris forrestii** Chinese pieris (red new growth)

*****Pieris japonica** lily-of-the-valley shrub (reddish new foliage)
    Cultivar: 'Variegata' (green and white).

*****Pittosporum tobira** Japanese pittosporum
    Cultivar: 'Variegata' (green and white).

Platycladus orientalis Oriental arborvitae
    Cultivars: *'Aurea Nana' (yellow) and *'Compacta' (gray-green).

Prunus × cistena purple-leaf sand cherry (purple)

*****Rosmarinus officinalis** rosemary (gray)

Taxus baccata English yew
    Cultivars: *'Aurea' (yellow) and *'Elegantissima' (green and yellow).

Taxus cuspidata Japanese yew
    Cultivar: *'Aurescens' (yellow).

Thuja occidentalis American arborvitae
    Cultivars: *'Aurea' (yellow), *'Lutea' (yellow), and *'Umbraculifera' (gray-blue).

Shrubs for Winter Interest

A shrub's structure, bark, stem, twigs, and buds offer delicate and subtle or bold and dramatic visual appeal to the winter landscape.

Acer palmatum var. dissectum laceleaf Japanese maple

Aronia arbutifolia red chokeberry

Cornus alba Tartarian dogwood

Corylus avellana 'Contorta' Harry Lauder's walkingstick

Cytisus × praecox Warminster broom

Genista species broom

Hamamelis species witchhazel

Ilex decidua deciduous holly, possumhaw

Ilex verticillata common winterberry

Kerria japonica Japanese rose

Lagerstroemia indica crapemyrtle

Magnolia species

Myrica pensylvanica northern bayberry

Rhus copallina flameleaf sumac, shining sumac

Rhus typhina staghorn sumac

Rosa hugonis Father Hugo rose

Rosa virginiana Virginia rose

Shrubs That Tolerate Shade

The following list includes shrubs that perform best in partial shade; the few that tolerate deep shade—regular but minimal sunlight—are marked with an asterisk (*).

Aesculus species horsechestnut, buckeye

*****Aucuba japonica** Japanese aucuba

Brunfelsia calycina

Calycanthus floridus Carolina allspice, strawberry-shrub

Camellia japonica common camellia

Chamaecyparis **species** false-cypress

Choisya ternata Mexican-orange

Clethra alnifolia summersweet, sweet pepperbush

Coprosma **species**

Cornus alba Tartarian dogwood

Euonymus **species** spindle tree

Ficus **species**

Fuchsia × *hybrida* common fuchsia

Fuchsia magellanica hardy fuchsia

Gardenia jasminoides gardenia

Hamamelis **species** witchhazel

Hydrangea **species**

Ilex **species** holly

Kalmia latifolia mountain-laurel

*Kerria japonica Japanese rose

Leucothoe fontanesiana drooping leucothoe

Ligustrum **species** privet

*Mahonia **species** oregongrape, hollygrape

Myrtus communis myrtle

Nandina domestica nandina, heavenly-bamboo

*Osmanthus **species** devilwood

Pieris **species**

Pittosporum **species**

Prunus laurocerasus English laurel

Rhododendron **species** rhododendron, azalea

Sarcococca **species** sweetbox

*Taxus **species** yew

Tsuga canadensis 'Pendula' Sargent's weeping hemlock

Viburnum × *juddii* Judd viburnum

Viburnum davidii David viburnum

Viburnum tinus laurustinus

Viburnum trilobum American cranberrybush viburnum

Shrubs for the Coldest Winters

Cold-hardy shrubs offer a variety of possibilities for the northern plains, mountains, or other northern latitudes. The following is only a partial list of those available. Each listing includes the coldest zone in which the shrub will thrive (see the Climate Zone Map on page 108).

Arctostaphylos uva-ursi kinnikinick (zone 2)

Caragana arborescens Siberian peashrub (zone 2)

Clethra alnifolia summersweet, sweet pepperbush (zone 3)

Cornus alba Tartarian dogwood (zone 2)

Genista tinctoria common woadwaxen (zone 2)

Ilex glabra inkberry (zone 3)

Juniperus communis common juniper (zone 2)

Juniperus horizontalis creeping juniper (zone 3)

Juniperus virginiana eastern redcedar (zone 2)

Lonicera tatarica Tartarian honeysuckle (zone 5)

Myrica pensylvanica northern bayberry (zone 5)

Picea **species** spruce (zone 2)

Pinus mugo var. *mugo* dwarf mountain pine (zone 2)

Potentilla fruticosa bush-cinquefoil (zone 2)

Prunus × *cistena* purple-leaf sand cherry (zone 2)

Prunus tomentosa Nanking cherry, Manchu cherry (zone 2)

Rhododendron canadense rhodora (zone 2)

Rhododendron lapponicum Lapland rhododendron (zone 3)

Rosa rubrifolia redleaf rose (zone 2)

Rosa rugosa rugosa rose, saltspray rose (zone 2)

Syringa vulgaris common lilac (zone 3B)

Tamarix ramosissima five-stamen tamarisk (zone 2)

Thuja occidentalis American arborvitae (zone 2)

Viburnum trilobum American cranberrybush viburnum (zone 3)

Drought-Tolerant Shrubs

In many parts of the United States, water is increasingly scarce. Where the water supply is more abundant, watering can be a time-consuming chore. Whether your garden is in the arid Southwest, the summer-drought climates of the West Coast, or the dry prairie states, planting shrubs from the following list can help conserve water and make gardening easier.

Arctostaphylos **species** manzanita

Aronia arbutifolia red chokeberry

Artemisia **species** artemisia, dustymiller

Aucuba japonica Japanese aucuba

Baccharis pilularis coyote brush

Berberis **species** barberry

Calliandra **species** fairy-duster, powderpuff

Callistemon citrinus lemon bottlebrush, crimson bottlebrush

Purple-leaf sand cherry (Prunus × cistena)

Caragana arborescens Siberian peashrub

Ceanothus species wild lilac

Cercis occidentalis western redbud

Cistus species rockrose

Coprosma species

Cotinus coggygria smoke tree

Cotoneaster species

Cytisus × praecox Warminster broom

Dodonaea viscosa hopbush

Elaeagnus species

Escallonia rubra red escallonia

Euonymus japonica evergreen euonymus, Japanese spindle tree

Feijoa sellowiana pineapple guava

Fremontodendron species fremontia

Genista species broom

Grevillea species spiderflower

Hypericum species St.-Johnswort

Juniperus species juniper

Lagerstroemia indica crapemyrtle

Lavandula species lavender

Leptospermum scoparium New Zealand tea-tree

Ligustrum species privet

Myrica pensylvanica northern bayberry

Myrtus communis myrtle

Nandina domestica nandina, heavenly-bamboo

Nerium oleander oleander

Osmanthus species sweet olive

Photinia species

Potentillia fruticosa bush-cinquefoil

Punica granatum pomegranate

Raphiolepis indica India-hawthorn

Rhus species sumac

Rosmarinus officinalis rosemary

Tamarix species tamarisk

Xylosma congestum shiny xylosma

Shrubs for City Dwellers

The following shrubs will adapt in areas of high pollution. Most of these are fairly tolerant of the restricted sunlight, reduced air circulation, and poor soils of the urban garden.

Aesculus parviflora bottlebrush buckeye

Arctostaphylos species manzanita

Aronia arbutifolia red chokeberry

Berberis thunbergii Japanese barberry

Caragana arborescens Siberian peashrub

Chaenomeles speciosa flowering quince

Cornus alba Tartarian dogwood

Cornus sericea redosier dogwood

Cotoneaster species cotoneaster

Elaeagnus species

Forsythia species

Hamamelis virginiana common witchhazel

Hibiscus rosa-sinensis Chinese hibiscus

Hibiscus syriacus shrub-althea, rose-of-Sharon

Hydrangea species

Hypericum species St.-Johnswort

Ilex crenata Japanese holly

Ilex glabra inkberry

Juniperus species juniper

Kerria japonica Japanese rose

Lagerstroemia indica crapemyrtle

Ligustrum species privet

Lonicera species honeysuckle

Magnolia stellata star magnolia

Mahonia aquifolium Oregon grapeholly

Malus sargentii Sargent's crabapple

Myrica pensylvanica northern bayberry

Nerium oleander oleander

Philadelphus coronarius sweet mockorange

Pittosporum tobira Japanese pittosporum

Potentilla fruticosa bush-cinquefoil

Pyracantha coccinea scarlet firethorn

Raphiolepis species hawthorn

Rhus species sumac

Ribes alpinum alpine currant

Rosa rugosa rugosa rose, saltspray rose

Rosa wichuraiana memorial rose

Spiraea × bumalda bumalda spirea

Spiraea × vanhouttei Vanhoutte spirea, bridalwreath

Syringa vulgaris common lilac

Taxus baccata English yew

Taxus cuspidata Japanese yew

Vaccinium corymbosum highbush blueberry

Viburnum opulus European cranberrybush

Shrubs With Fall Foliage Color

Many deciduous shrubs are very striking in the fall when their foliage changes shades. Frequently, their colors are brighter and longer lasting than many flowers. Consult the list that follows for some of the more spectacular choices.

Abelia × grandiflora glossy abelia

Acer palmatum var. *dissectum* laceleaf Japanese maple

Broom (Genista species)

Silverberry 'maculata' (Elaeagnus pungens 'Maculata')

Staghorn sumac (Rhus typhina)

Aronia arbutifolia   red chokeberry
Berberis thunbergii   Japanese barberry
Clethra alnifolia   summersweet, sweet pepperbush
Cornus alba   Tartarian dogwood
Cornus sericea   redosier dogwood
Cotinus coggygria   smoke tree
Cotoneaster divaricatus   spreading cotoneaster
Cotoneaster horizontalis   rock cotoneaster
Enkianthus campanulatus   redvein enkianthus
Euonymus alata   burning-bush, winged euonymus
Fothergilla major   large fothergilla
Hamamelis species   witchhazel

Hydrangea quercifolia   oakleaf hydrangea
Lagerstroemia indica   crapemyrtle
Mahonia aquifolium   Oregon grapeholly
Nandina domestica   nandina, heavenly-bamboo
Paxistima canbyi   Canby paxistima, cliffgreen
Punica granatum   pomegranate
Rhododendron arborescens   sweet azalea
Rhododendron kaempferi   torch azalea
Rhododendron Knapp Hill–Exbury azalea hybrids
Rhododendron schlippenbachii   royal azalea
Rhododendron vaseyi   pinkshell azalea
Rhus species   sumac
Rosa virginiana   Virginia rose
Vaccinium corymbosum   highbush blueberry
Viburnum × carlcephalum   fragrant snowball viburnum
Viburnum × juddii   Judd viburnum
Viburnum dilatatum   linden viburnum
Viburnum opulus   European cranberrybush
Viburnum plicatum var. **tomentosum**   doublefile viburnum
Viburnum trilobum   American cranberrybush viburnum

Shrubs With Fragrant Flowers

Many shrubs in the Plant Selection Guide are fragrant, but the ones listed below have the most powerful and pleasant scents. Plant fragrance is usually most intense on days that are humid and mild, especially during early to mid-morning and evening hours.

Boronia species
Buddleia davidii   summer lilac, orange-eye buddleia
Calycanthus floridus   Carolina allspice, strawberry-shrub
Cestrum species
Choisya ternata   Mexican-orange
Clethra alnifolia   summersweet, sweet pepperbush
Cytisus battandieri   Morocco broom
Daphne species
Elaeagnus species
Fothergilla major   large fothergilla
Gardenia jasminoides   gardenia
Hamamelis species   witchhazel
Lavandula species   lavender
Leucothoe fontanesiana   drooping leucothoe
Lonicera species   honeysuckle
Magnolia stellata   star magnolia
Michelia species
Osmanthus species   devilwood
Philadelphus species   mockorange
Pittosporum napaulense   golden-fragrance plant
Pittosporum tobira   Japanese pittosporum
Prunus tomentosa   Nanking cherry, Manchu cherry
Rhododendron × loderi   loderi hybrid rhododendron
Rhododendron arborescens   sweet azalea
Rhododendron periclymenoides   pinxterbloom azalea
Rhododendron viscosum   swamp azalea
Rosa spinosissima   Scotch rose
Rosa wichuraiana   memorial rose
Sarcococca species   sweetbox
Syringa vulgaris   common lilac
Viburnum species   viburnum

Escallonia (Escallonia × fradessi)

Linden viburnum (Viburnum dilatatum)

Fast-Growing Shrubs

The shrubs listed below grow more quickly than most, although most still take at least two seasons before they resemble a mature effect. Choosing a plant for the speed at which it reaches maturity involves compromise. In general, the faster-growing shrubs have shorter lives and must be replaced more frequently.

Abelia × grandiflora glossy abelia
***Berberis* species** barberry
Callistemon citrinus lemon bottlebrush, crimson bottlebrush
Caragana arborescens Siberian peashrub
***Ceanothus* species** wild lilac
Choisya ternata Mexican-orange
***Cistus* species** rockrose
***Coprosma* species**
Cornus alba Tartarian dogwood
Cornus sericea redosier dogwood
Cotoneaster dammeri bearberry cotoneaster
Cotoneaster divaricatus spreading cotoneaster
Cytisus × praecox Warminster broom
***Elaeagnus* species**
***Escallonia* species**
***Forsythia* species**
Fuchsia × hybrida common fuchsia
Hydrangea macrophylla bigleaf hydrangea, French hydrangea

Hypericum calycinum Aaron's-beard, St.-Johnswort
Kerria japonica Japanese rose
Kolkwitzia amabilis beautybush
***Ligustrum* species** privet
***Lonicera* species** honeysuckle
***Myrica* species** bayberry
Nerium oleander oleander
***Philadelphus* species** mockorange
***Pittosporum* species** pittosporum
***Pyracantha* species** firethorn
Rhus copallina flameleaf sumac, shining sumac
Rhus typhina staghorn sumac
***Rosa* species** rose
***Spirea* species** spirea
***Tamarix* species** tamarisk, saltcedar
Weigela florida old-fashioned weigela

Shrubs That Attract Birds

Nearly all shrubs, except for the low dwarfs, provide attractive habitats and protection for birds. The ones on this list provide an especially valuable nesting or hiding environment, or edible fruits in different seasons.

***Arctostaphylos* species** manzanita
Aronia arbutifolia red chokeberry
***Berberis* species** barberry
***Buddleia* species** butterfly bush
Callistemon citrinus lemon bottlebrush, crimson bottlebrush
***Ceanothus* species** wild lilac
***Cornus* species** dogwood

***Cotoneaster* species** cotoneaster
***Elaeagnus* species**
***Escallonia* species**
***Fuchsia* species**
***Ilex* species** holly
***Juniperus* species** juniper
***Ligustrum* species** privet
***Lonicera* species** honeysuckle
***Mahonia* species** oregongrape, hollygrape
Malus sargentii Sargent's crabapple
Myrica pensylvanica northern bayberry
***Photinia* species**
***Prunus* species**
***Pyracantha* species** firethorn
Rhamnus alaternus Italian buckthorn
***Rhus* species** sumac
***Rosa* species** rose
***Rosmarinus* species** rosemary
Symplocos paniculata sapphire-berry, Asiatic sweetleaf
***Vaccinium* species** blueberry, huckleberry
***Viburnum* species**

Shrubs for Containers

Some shrubs adapt more easily to container culture than others. The shrubs that usually do best in containers already have a naturally neat and compact growth habit or can easily be kept that way. Use the following list as a guide for adding greenery and color to a deck or patio. Also see the list of dwarf shrubs on page 62 for more ideas about shrubs that are suitable for container gardening.

Acer palmatum* var. *dissectum laceleaf Japanese maple
Aucuba japonica Japanese aucuba
Buxus microphylla littleleaf boxwood
Buxus sempervirens common boxwood
***Camellia* species**
***Chamaecyparis* species** false-cypress
***Corylus avellana* 'Contorta'** Harry Lauder's walkingstick
Cotoneaster horizontalis rock cotoneaster

Dwarf pomegranate (Punica granatum)

Euonymus fortunei winter-creeper
Fuchsia × hybrida common fuchsia
Gardenia jasminoides gardenia
Hydrangea macrophylla bigleaf hydrangea, French hydrangea
Ilex cornuta Chinese holly
Ilex crenata Japanese holly
Ilex vomitoria 'Nana' yaupon
Kalmia latifolia mountain-laurel
Lagerstroemia indica crapemyrtle
Leptospermum scoparium New Zealand tea-tree
Leucothoe fontanesiana drooping leucothoe
Ligustrum species privet
Lonicera nitida box honeysuckle
Mahonia bealei leatherleaf mahonia
Mahonia lomariifolia
Myrtus communis myrtle
Nandina domestica nandina, heavenly-bamboo
Nerium oleander oleander
Osmanthus species devilwood
Picea species spruce (dwarf varieties)
Pieris japonica lily-of-the-valley-bush
Pinus pine (dwarf varieties)
Pittosporum tobira Japanese pittosporum
Prunus laurocerasus English laurel
Punica granatum pomegranate
Pyracantha species firethorn
Raphiolepis indica India-hawthorn

Rhododendron species rhododendron and azalea
Rosmarinus officinalis rosemary
Taxus species yew
Thuja species arborvitae (dwarf varieties)
Tsuga canadensis 'Pendula' Sargent's weeping hemlock

Thorny Shrubs for Barriers

Thorny shrubs are difficult to work with. Use them for their value as barriers, planting them where they will not scratch passers-by or interfere with garden activities. The following shrubs provides an impenetrable barrier.

Berberis species barberry
Carissa species carissa
Chaenomeles speciosa common flowering quince
Elaeagnus pungens silverberry
Hakea suaveolens pincushion-tree
Ilex cornuta Chinese holly
Mahonia species
Osmanthus heterophyllus holly olive
Poncirus trifoliatus trifoliate-orange, hardy-orange
Pyracantha coccinea scarlet firethorn
Ribes speciosum fuchsia-flowered gooseberry
Rosa species rose

Shrubs for Acid Soils

While most shrubs will tolerate a moderately acid soil (pH 6), many require acid soil to thrive. Consider the following only if you have, or can maintain, soil with a pH of 6 or less.

Arctostaphylos uva-ursi kinnikinick
Calluna vulgaris Scotch heather
Camellia species
Choisya ternata Mexican orange
Clethra alnifolia summersweet, sweet pepperbush
Enkianthus campanulatus redvein enkianthus
Erica species heath
Exochorda species pearlbush
Fothergilla species fothergilla
Gardenia jasminoides gardenia

Fuchsia-flowered gooseberry (Ribes speciosum)

Redvein enkianthus (Enkianthus campanulatus)

Hydrangea quercifolia oakleaf hydrangea
Ilex species holly
Juniperus communis common juniper
Kalmia latifolia mountain-laurel
Leucothoe fontanesiana drooping leucothoe
Magnolia species magnolia
Mahonia species
Paxistima canbyi Canby paxistima, cliffgreen
Rhododendron species rhododendron, azalea
Tsuga canadensis 'Pendula' Sargent's weeping hemlock
Vaccinium corymbosum highbush blueberry

Inkberry (Ilex glabra)

Goldflower St.-Johnswort (Hypericum × moseranum)

Shrubs for Wet Soils

For many gardeners, working with heavy, poorly draining soil is a serious problem. Often, low spots collect water, which remains for a long time. The following list contains shrubs that perform well in standing water, along with other plants that tolerate a low amount of soil aeration.

Aronia arbutifolia   red chokeberry
Calycanthus floridus   Carolina allspice, strawberry-shrub
Clethra alnifolia   summersweet, sweet pepperbush
Cornus alba   Tartarian dogwood
Cornus sericea   redosier dogwood
Hamamelis vernalis   vernal witchhazel
Hypericum densiflorum   dense hypericum
Ilex glabra   inkberry
Ilex verticillata   common winterberry
Myrica pensylvanica   northern bayberry
Potentilla fruticosa   bush-cinquefoil
Rhododendron canadense   rhodora
Rhododendron viscosum   swamp azalea
Viburnum cassinoides   withe-rod viburnum
Viburnum opulus   European cranberrybush
Viburnum trilobum   American cranberrybush viburnum

Shrubs for Ground Covers

Many woody shrubs make excellent ground covers. The selections that follow represent the best of the low, spreading forms. Consider them for covering a steep bank where a lawn is difficult to maintain and where a solution to erosion is needed. Some of them do well in large beds. In addition to the plants listed below, the list of dwarf shrubs on page 62 includes plants that are suitable for ground covers.

Abelia × grandiflora 'Prostrata'
Arctostaphylos hookeri   Hooker manzanita
Arctostaphylos uva-ursi   kinnikinick
Baccharis pilularis   coyotebrush, chaparral-broom
Berberis thunbergii   Japanese barberry (selected varieties)
Calluna vulgaris   Scotch heather
Ceanothus   wild lilac (selected varieties)
Chaenomeles (selected varieties)
***Cistus* species**   rockrose
Coprosma × kirkii
Cotoneaster dammeri   bearberry cotoneaster
Cotoneaster horizontalis   rock cotoneaster
***Erica* species**   heath
***Helianthemum* species**   sun rose
Hypericum calycinum   Aaron's-beard, St.-Johnswort

Iberis sempervirens   evergreen candytuft
Ilex glabra 'Compacta'
Juniperus chinensis   Chinese juniper (selected varieties)
Juniperus chinensis procumbens   Japanese garden juniper
Juniperus horizontalis   creeping juniper
Juniperus sabina   savin juniper (selected varieties)
Leptospermum scoparium   New Zealand tea-tree (selected varieties)
Leucothoe fontanesiana   drooping leucothoe
Lonicera × xylosteoides 'Clavey's Dwarf'
Myoporum parviflorum 'Putah Creek'
Paxistima canbyi   Canby paxistima, cliffgreen
Pyracantha coccinea   scarlet firethorn
Ribes viburnifolium
Rosa wichuraiana   memorial rose
Rosmarinus officinalis   rosemary
***Santolina* species**   lavender-cotton

Shrubs With Showy Fruit

Although shrub flowers often last only a week or so, the brightly colored fruits of many shrubs could last an entire winter. The following list presents some of the more beautiful ornamental and fruited shrubs.

***Arctostaphylos* species**   manzanita
Aronia arbutifolia   red chokeberry
Aucuba japonica   Japanese aucuba
Berberis darwinii   Darwin barberry
Berberis koreana   Korean barberry
Berberis thunbergii   Japanese barberry
Chaenomeles speciosa   common flowering quince
Cotoneaster dammeri   bearberry cotoneaster
Cotoneaster divaricatus   spreading cotoneaster
Cotoneaster horizontalis   rock cotoneaster
Cotoneaster multiflorus   many-flowered cotoneaster

Nandina, heavenly-bamboo (Nandina domestica)

***Elaeagnus* species**
Euonymus fortunei winter-creeper (selected varieties)
Ilex cornuta Chinese holly
Ilex decidua possumhaw
Ilex verticillata common winterberry
Ilex vomitoria yaupon
Lonicera tatarica Tartarian honeysuckle
***Mahonia* species** oregongrape, hollygrape
Malus sargentii Sargent's crabapple
Myrica pensylvanica northern bayberry
Nandina domestica nandina, heavenly-bamboo
***Photinia* species**
Prunus maritima beach plum
Prunus tomentosa Nanking cherry, Manchu cherry
Punica granatum pomegranate
Pyracantha coccinea scarlet firethorn
Rhus copallina flameleaf sumac, shining sumac
Rhus typhina staghorn sumac
Rosa hugonis Father Hugo rose
Rosa virginiana Virginia rose
Symplocos paniculata sapphire-berry, Asiatic sweetleaf
Vaccinium corymbosum highbush blueberry
Viburnum* × *juddii Judd viburnum
Viburnum davidii David viburnum

Viburnum dilatatum linden viburnum
Viburnum opulus European cranberrybush
Viburnum plicatum* var. *tomentosum doublefile viburnum
Viburnum tinus lautustinus
Viburnum trilobum American cranberrybush viburnum

Shrubs That Are Easy to Care For

Most shrubs are easy to maintain once the correct conditions for growth are met. However, knowing and creating those conditions may be difficult. The shrubs listed here adapt to a wide variety of conditions and are pest resistant.

Abelia* × *grandiflora glossy abelia
Aesculus parviflora bottlebrush buckeye
Arctostaphylos uva-ursi kinnikinick
Aronia arbutifolia red chokeberry
Aucuba japonica Japanese aucuba
***Berberis* species** barberry
Callistemon citrinus lemon bottlebrush, crimson bottlebrush
Calycanthus floridus Carolina allspice, strawberry-shrub
Caragana arborescens Siberian peashrub
Chaenomeles speciosa common flowering quince
***Cistus* species** rockrose
Clethra alnifolia summersweet, sweet pepperbush
***Coprosma* species**
Cornus alba Tartarian dogwood
Cornus sericea redosier dogwood
***Corylus avellana* 'Contorta'** Harry Lauder's walkingstick
Cotinus coggygria smoke tree
***Cotoneaster* species** cotoneaster
***Cytisus* species** broom
***Deutzia* species**
***Elaeagnus* species**
Euonymus alata burning-bush, winged euonymus
***Exochorda* species** pearlbush
Fothergilla major large fothergilla
***Genista* species** broom

***Hamamelis* species** witchhazel
***Hypericum* species** St.-Johnswort
***Ilex* species** holly
***Juniperus* species** juniper
Kerria japonica Japanese rose
Kolkwitzia amabilis beautybush
Lagerstroemia indica crapemyrtle
Leptospermum scoparium New Zealand tea-tree
***Ligustrum* species** privet
Lonicera* × *xylosteoides
Lonicera nitida box honeysuckle
Malus sargentii Sargent's crabapple
Myrica pensylvanica northern bayberry
Myrtus communis myrtle
Nandina domestica nandina, heavenly-bamboo
Nerium oleander oleander
***Osmanthus* species** devilwood
Paxistima canbyi Canby paxistima, cliffgreen
***Philadelphus* species** mockorange
***Pinus* species** pine
***Pittosporum* species**
Potentilla fruticosa bush-cinquefoil
Prunus* × *cistena purple-leaf sand cherry
Prunus tomentosa Nanking cherry, Manchu cherry
Raphiolepis indica India-hawthorn
***Rhus* species** sumac
***Rosa* species** rose
Rosmarinus officinalis rosemary
***Spiraea* species** spirea
Symplocos paniculata sapphire-berry, Asiatic sweetleaf
***Taxus* species** yew
***Thuja* species** arborvitae
***Viburnum* species**
Xylosma congestum shiny xylosma

Shrubs for Hedges and Other Formal Shapes

Consider the following shrubs when planning a hedge, topiary, or other formal design—all take close shearing and clipping well.

Abelia* × *grandiflora glossy abelia
Berberis thunbergii Japanese barberry
***Buxus* species** boxwood

Rugosa rose, saltspray rose (Rosa rugosa)

Dwarf yaupon (Ilex vomitoria)

***Chamaecyparis* species**   false-cypress
Elaeagnus pungens   silverberry
Euonymus fortunei   winter-creeper (shrub cultivars)
Euonymus kiautschovicus   spreading euonymus
Euonymus japonica   evergreen euonymus, Japanese spindle tree
Ilex cornuta   Chinese holly (small cultivars)
Ilex crenata   Japanese holly
Ilex glabra   inkberry
Ilex vomitoria   yaupon
***Juniperus* species**   juniper (selected cultivars)
***Ligustrum* species**   privet
Lonicera × xylosteoides
Lonicera nitida   box honeysuckle
Myrtus communis   myrtle
***Osmanthus* species**   devilwood
Pittosporum crassifolium   karo
Pittosporum eugenoides   tarata
Prunus laurocerasus   English laurel
Prunus tomentosa   Nanking cherry, Manchu cherry
Pyracantha coccinea   scarlet firethorn
Rhododendron maximum   rosebay rhododendron
Rosmarinus officinalis   rosemary
***Taxus* species**   yew
Viburnum tinus   lautustinus
Xylosma congestum   shiny xylosma

Shrubs for the Seacoast

Seacoast gardens have their own unique problems ranging from harsh, constant winds to sandy soil and salt spray. The plants in the list below perform well under these conditions. Usually, they also make excellent choices for desert gardens.

***Arctostaphylos* species**   manzanita
Callistemon citrinus   lemon bottlebrush, crimson bottlebrush
***Calocephalus* species**
***Carissa* species**
***Ceanothus* species**   wild lilac
***Cistus* species**   rockrose
***Coprosma* species**
Cotoneaster dammeri   bearberry cotoneaster
Cotoneaster divaricatus   spreading cotoneaster
Cotoneaster horizontalis   rock cotoneaster
Cytisus × praecox   Warminster broom
***Elaeagnus* species**
***Escallonia* species**
***Genista* species**   broom
***Grevillea* species**   spiderflower
***Hakea* species**   pincushion-tree
Hibiscus syriacus   shrub-althea, rose-of-Sharon
Hydrangea macrophylla   bigleaf hydrangea, French hydrangea
***Juniperus* species**   juniper (especially *J. conferta*, shore juniper)

Leptospermum scoparium   New Zealand tea-tree
***Leucodendron* species**
Lonicera nitida   box honeysuckle
***Melaleuca* species**   bottlebrush
Myrica pensylvanica   northern bayberry
Pittosporum crassifolium   karo
***Protea* species**
Prunus maritima   beach plum
Raphiolepis indica   India-hawthorn
Rosa rugosa   rugosa rose, saltspray rose
Rosa virginiana   Virginia rose
Rosmarinus officinalis   rosemary
***Tamarix* species**   tamarisk, saltcedar

Dwarf Shrubs

The shrubs in the following list are small and generally slow growing, with mature heights of 3 feet or less under normal growing conditions. The list does not include dwarf shrubs created by pruning and restricting root growth—such as container, bonsai, and topiary plants—or by grafting. Dwarf shrubs are useful where garden space is at a premium and are excellent in foundation plantings, on steep banks, or as edging along drives, walks, borders, and beds. See page 23 for more on dwarf shrubs. An asterisk (*) indicates widespreading and rapid-growing shrubs that are suitable for ground covers.

***Abelia × grandiflora* 'Prostrata'**
Andromeda polifolia   bog-rosemary
Arctostaphylos uva-ursi   kinnikinick
****Berberis darwinii* 'Corallina Compacta'**
***Berberis thunbergii* 'Crimson Pigmy'**
***Buxus microphylla* var. *koreana* 'Tide Hill'**
Buxus sempervirens   common boxwood
   Cultivars: 'Bullata', 'Suffruticosa', and 'Vardar Valley'.
Calluna vulgaris   Scotch heather
***Caragana arborescens* 'Nana'**
Ceanothus gloriosus   Point Reyes ceanothus
Ceanothus griseus var. *horizontalis   Carmel creeper

Chamaecyparis lawsoniana
Lawson false-cypress
   Cultivars: 'Minima Glauca' and 'Nidiformis'.
Chamaecyparis obtusa Hinoki false-cypress
   Cultivars: 'Kosteri', 'Lycopioides', and 'Nana'.
Chamaecyparis pisifera 'Squarrosa Minima'
Coprosma × kirkii
Cornus sericea 'Isanti'
Cotoneaster dammeri bearberry cotoneaster
Cotoneaster horizontalis rock cotoneaster
   Cultivars: 'Little Gem' and 'Perpusilla'.
Daphne cneorum garlandflower
Erica carnea spring heath
Erica vagans Cornish heath
Euonymus fortunei winter-creeper
   Cultivars: 'Azusa', 'Emerald Cushion', and 'Kewensis'.
Euonymus fortunei var. *colorata*
Euonymus japonica evergreen euonymus, Japanese spindle tree
   Cultivars: 'Microphylla' and 'Microphylla Variegata'.
Fothergilla gardenii dwarf fothergilla
Fuchsia × hybrida common fuchsia
Gardenia jasminoides 'Radicans'
Genista pilosa silkyleaf woadwaxen
Genista sagittalis arrow broom
Genista tinctoria common woadwaxen
Hypericum calycinum Aaron's-beard, St.-Johnswort
Hypericum frondosum 'Sunburst'
Iberis sempervirens evergreen candytuft
Ilex cornuta Chinese holly
   Cultivars: 'Berries Jubilee', 'Carissa', 'Dazzler', and 'Dwarf Burford'.
Ilex crenata Japanese holly
   Cultivars: 'Border Gem', 'Golden Gem', 'Green Island', and 'Kingsville Green Cushion'.
Ilex vomitoria 'Nana' yaupon

Juniperus chinensis Chinese juniper
   Cultivars: 'Alba', 'Armstrong', 'Blue Vase', 'Fruitland', 'Mint Julep', 'Pfitzeriana Arctic', and 'Pfitzeriana Kallay'.
Juniperus chinensis procumbens Japanese garden juniper
   Cultivar: 'Nana'.
Juniperus chinensis var. *sargentii*
   Cultivars: 'Compacta', 'Glauca', and 'Viridis'.
Juniperus communis common juniper
   Cultivars: 'Compressa', *'Depressa', 'Gold Beach', and 'Hornibrookii'.
Juniperus conferta shore juniper
   Cultivars: 'Blue Pacific' and 'Emerald Sea'.
Juniperus horizontalis creeping juniper
Juniperus sabina savin juniper
   Cultivars: 'Arcadia', 'Broadmoor', *'Buffalo', and 'Skandia'.
Juniperus sabina var. *tamariscifolia*
Juniperus virginiana 'Silver Spreader'
Lagerstroemia indica crapemyrtle (petite series)
Leptospermum scoparium New Zealand tea-tree
   Cultivars: 'Horizontalis', 'Nanum', 'Snow White', and 'Waeringi'.
Leucothoe fontanesiana 'Nana'
Lonicera × xylosteoides
   Cultivars: 'Clavey's Dwarf' and 'Emerald Mound'.
Lonicera tatarica Tartarian honeysuckle
   Cultivars: 'Nana' and 'LeRoyana'.
Myrtus communis myrtle
   Cultivars: 'Compacta', 'Compacta Variegata', and 'Microphylla'.
Paxistima canbyi Canby paxistima, cliffgreen
Pieris japonica lily-of-the-valley shrub
   Cultivars: 'Crispa' and 'Pygmaea'.
Pinus mugo var. *mugo* dwarf mountain pine
   Cultivars: 'Compacta', 'Gnome', and 'Slavinii'.

Pittosporum tobira 'Wheeler's Dwarf'
Platycladus orientalis oriental arborvitae
   Cultivars: 'Aurea Nana', 'Bonita', and 'Raffles'.
Potentilla fruticosa bush-cinquefoil
Prunus laurocerasus English laurel
   Cultivars: 'Mt. Vernon', 'Nana', and 'Otto Luyken'.
Punica granatum pomegranate
   Cultivars: 'Chico' and 'Nana'.
Pyracantha species firethorn
   Cultivars: 'Red Elf', and 'Tiny Tim'.
Raphiolepis indica India-hawthorn
Rhododendron canadense rhodora
Rhododendron impeditum cloudland rhododendron
Rhododendron lapponicum Lapland rhododendron
Rosmarinus officinalis rosemary
   Cultivars: *'Collingwood Ingram' and *'Prostratus'.
Spiraea × bumalda bumalda spirea
Spiraea albiflora Japanese white spirea
Spiraea japonica 'Alpina'
Taxus × media 'Berryhilli'
Taxus baccata English yew
   Cultivars: 'Nana', 'Pygmaea', and 'Repandens'.
Taxus cuspidata Japanese yew
   Cultivars: 'Aurescens', 'Densa', 'Intermedia', and 'Nana'.
Thuja occidentalis American arborvitae
   Cultivars: 'Aurea', Boothii', 'Ericoides', 'Little Gem', and 'Umbraculifera'.
Viburnum davidii David viburnum
Viburnum opulus European cranberrybush
   Cultivars: 'Compactum' and 'Nanum'.
Viburnum trilobum 'Compactum'
Weigela florida old-fashioned weigela
   Cultivars: 'Foliis Purpuriis' and 'Variegata Nana'.
Xylosma congestum 'Compacta'

Abelia × *grandiflora* (glossy abelia)

Aesculus parviflora (bottlebrush buckeye)

A GALLERY OF SHRUBS

When selecting a shrub, no description or photograph can take the place of seeing a live, healthy, and mature plant. The following guide provides a brief introduction to a wide variety of shrubs. As you find shrubs of interest in this guide, try to locate a mature, healthy example. Talk with friends who have grown the shrub or with your local garden center. Trained nursery staff have experience with many shrubs, including hearing customer experiences with different shrubs. Take advantage of this knowledge to learn about local shrub adaptation and uses not discussed in the following descriptions.

Abelia × grandiflora

Glossy abelia
Zones 6 to 10
Broad-leafed evergreen
(deciduous in the North)
This hybrid makes an effective specimen, informal hedge, grouping, or mass, combining particularly well with broad-leafed evergreens. Showy, pinkish white flowers cover the plant from July until frost. Finely textured, glossy, deep green summer foliage turns an attractive bronze in the fall. It is deciduous to semievergreen in the north and increasingly evergreen the farther south it is grown. The habit is graceful, rounded, and arching. It grows at a medium to fast rate, reaching 4 to 8 feet high and wide. Give it well-drained soil, half to full sun, and average watering, and it will prove to be an easy-to-grow and, pest-free plant. Although it easily can be sheared into formal shapes, doing so seriously reduces flowering. It is probably best to allow it to achieve its natural, graceful shape. Expect frequent winter dieback in northern zone 6, although the new growth comes back quickly. Older, overgrown shrubs can be renewed by cutting back in late winter or early spring. Lower, spreading forms, such as 'Prostrata' and 'Sherwoodii', make excellent, large-scale ground covers.

Acer palmatum var. dissectum

Laceleaf Japanese maple
Zones 6 to 10
Deciduous
This is a dwarf tree providing a refined, aristocratic touch. An open, picturesque form; growing quite slowly 6 to 8 feet in height and width; soft, wispy foliage available in a variety of shades and variegations; and consistently showy fall color all make this an outstanding specimen plant. Consider using it as a focal point for an entryway, or naturalized in a woodland understory. In containers, it makes an excellent bonsai subject.

In zone 6 the roots of container plants should be given extra protection in the winter—mulch and add extra insulation to the container, or sink it into the ground in a protected spot. Transplant from a container in winter or early spring into well-drained, acid soil (pH 5.5 to 6.5) that is rich in organic matter. Filtered shade, especially in hot climates, as well as protection from drying winds—especially the cold, drying winds and late frosts of spring are preferable due to this plant's susceptibility to leaf scorch.

Not all varieties of Japanese maple are the laceleaf dwarfs. Some are 15- to 25-foot trees with an extensive range of different foliage qualities. If a shrublike plant is desired, always ask for the laceleaf types. Some of the better cultivars are 'Crimson King', 'Garnet', 'Flavescens', 'Ornatum', 'Ozakazuki', 'Purpureum', 'Reticulatum', and 'Sangokaku'. Native to Japan, China, and Korea.

Aesculus parviflora

Bottlebrush buckeye
Zones 5 to 8
Deciduous
Spectacular late-season flowers, trouble-free foliage (unusual for the buckeyes), and adaptability to heavy shade make this shrub an excellent specimen, massing and clumping in shady areas, such as under large shade trees. Not a shrub for small areas, its open, wide-spreading (8 to 15 feet) suckering habit can be

Aronia arbutifolia (red chokeberry)

Aucuba japonica (Japanese aucuba)

Aesculus pavia (red buckeye)

troublesome if not given room to grow. The flowers are profuse, large, erect clusters that grow 8 to 12 inches long, are white with red anthers, and bloom from early to late July. *Aesculus parviflora* prefers moist, well-drained soil high in organic matter, and it tolerates full sun to heavy shade. 'Roger's' is a superior cultivar that produces flower clusters 18 to 24 inches long. Native to moist woods from South Carolina to Alabama.

Aesculus pavia (red buckeye, zones 6 to 8)   Like bottlebrush buckeye, this shrub is relatively resistant to most leaf diseases that plague the buckeyes. Mildew does not affect this shrub's long-term vigor. Red buckeye differs largely from bottlebrush buckeye by having bright red flowers in early spring and being less hardy. In size and form it is much the same. *A. pavia* 'Atrosanguinea' has darker red flowers, while 'Humilis' is a low, often prostrate form. Native to the coastal plain woods, from southeast Virginia to Florida, west to Texas, and north to southern Illinois.

Arctostaphylos uva-ursi

Bearberry manzanita, kinnikinick
Zones 2 to 8A
Broad-leafed evergreen

A low, mat-forming ground cover with evergreen foliage of pleasing, fine texture, bearberry manzanita is especially useful for poor, sandy soil. Drooping, tiny, bell-shaped flowers are followed by bright red berries. Set these relatively slow-growing plants from containers or flats 2 feet apart for complete cover in about two seasons. Bearberry is salt tolerant and therefore makes an excellent beach plant. It is native to northern and arctic Europe, Asia, and North America, where it is found south to Virginia, northern Mexico, and northern California. In addition to *Arctostaphylos uva-ursi*, over 60 species of *Arctostaphylos* are native to western North America, from southern California to British Columbia. Most are large (10 to 20 feet), open shrubs with gnarled, smooth trunks, vivid red bark,

and grayish green to deep green leathery, evergreen foliage. They have mildly to quite showy white to deep pink clusters of flowers. Useful as drought-tolerant natives in gardens west of the Rockies, all are quite particular as to soil and habitat. Check with your local nursery for the species and cultivar that is best suited to your garden.

Aronia arbutifolia

Red chokeberry
Zones 5 to 8
Deciduous

In addition to displaying spectacular bright red berries in profusion and red to purple fall color, the red chokeberry is easy to grow. A distinctly leggy, upright shrub that grows slowly 6 to 10 feet high and 3 to 5 feet wide, this plant is best used in masses and large groups that serve to accentuate the fruit display and diminish its legginess. Naturalized at the edge of woodlands and around ponds and other wet areas, a large planting is like an ocean of red in fall and winter. Although it

is an excellent choice for that problem wet area, and although it performs well in heavy soil, it is also tolerant of dry soils and prairie drought. Fruiting is best in full sun. Adaptable and little troubled by pests, the red chokeberry is a carefree plant. Native to thickets in bogs, swamps, wet woods, and occasionally dry soils from Nova Scotia to Florida, and west to Michigan, Missouri, and Texas.

Aucuba japonica

Japanese aucuba
Zones 7B to 10
Broad-leafed evergreen

Valued for its tolerance of heavy shade, for its leathery, large, evergreen leaves, and for its adaptability to adverse growing conditions, the Japanese aucuba also makes an excellent container plant. Use it in shady areas, such as a dim, north-facing entryway, or under densely foliaged trees (it competes well with tree roots). Unpruned, the shrub becomes a leggy, open plant that grows 6 to over 10 feet tall. Prune to

Berberis koreana (Korean barberry)

Berberis darwinii (Darwin barberry)

Berberis thunbergii 'Atropurpurea' (Japanese barberry)

keep it a dense, rounded shrub by selectively cutting branches back to a leaf node. Bright red berries can be attractive in the fall and winter, but both male and female plants are needed in order to set fruit. Performing well in any soil, and drought tolerant once established, Japanese aucuba still benefits from additional organic matter in the soil at the time it is planted. This is not a plant for hot, sunny, exposed locations. Native from the Himalayas to Japan. Numerous cultivars are available for different foliage colors, variegations, and shapes.

Berberis darwinii

Darwin barberry
Zones 8 to 10
Broad-leafed evergreen

This is the showiest barberry in flower, producing masses of bright, yellow-orange flowers in early March. It grows rapidly into an arching, loose shrub, 5 to 10 feet high and 4 to 7 feet wide, with small, evergreen leaves. Its dark blue berries are beautiful and attract birds. It has a tendency to spread by underground stolons, and becomes loose and open in old age unless pruned regularly. Like all barberries, it is not particular to soil and withstands drought well. 'Corallina Compacta' is especially valuable for its neat, dense, compact, and rounded shape. Native to Chile.

Berberis koreana

Korean barberry
Zones 5 to 8
Deciduous

This is the showiest hardy barberry for flower and fruit, bearing yellow flowers in 3- to 4-inch-long drooping racemes from early to mid-May, followed by profuse, bright red berries that persist well into winter. Like the Japanese barberry, it makes an excellent thorny barrier, and is adaptable and trouble-free. Individual plants grow to a dense oval 4 to 6 feet high with slightly less spread. Suckers spread prolifically from the roots, occasionally forming large colonies. It is best reserved for large informal hedges and borders. Native to Korea.

Berberis thunbergii

Japanese barberry
Zones 5 to 9
Deciduous

The Japanese barberry is one of the most popular hedge and barrier plants. It is easy to grow, and has impenetrable thorns and dense, shearable foliage. Outstanding fall color and mildly effective winter fruits are features, as are the numerous red-, yellow-, and variegated-leafed cultivars. The plant collects trash, which is particularly unattractive in winter. The sharp thorns make removal of accumulated trash very difficult. The thorns also cause trouble for weeding or other gardening near the plant. It grows at a moderate rate to 3 to 6 feet high and 4 to 7 feet wide. The natural outline of this shrub is upright, arching, and rounded, with a dense profusion of thorny stems and finely textured foliage. Easily transplanted, this barberry is adaptable to nearly any soil, withstands drought well, and performs in full sun or partial shade. Cultivars with colored foliage generally retain their color only if grown in full sun. The cultivar 'Crimson Pygmy' makes a good ground cover for a hot, sunny area, as well as a low hedge. Native from southern Europe across Asia to central China and the Himalayas.

Buddleia davidii

Butterfly bush
Zones 5 to 10
Deciduous

A favorite for attractive, fragrant, midsummer flowers that draw butterflies, this shrub is wild and unruly in its growth habit. With extremely large leaves and coarse texture, it grows rapidly to an open, rangy 6 to 10 feet. The flowers are fragrant, 6- to 12-inch-long spikes that appear in July and August. Treat this shrub as an herbaceous perennial in the rear of a perennial border, pruning it after it flowers each fall to within a few inches of the ground. This helps to keep it manageable and increases the number of flowering shoots. While *Buddleia* is susceptible to

Buxus sempervirens (common boxwood)

Calluna vulgaris (Scotch heather)

many different pests, spraying for them also eliminates the visitation of any butterflies. Numerous cultivars are available for flower color, ranging from white through pinks and reds to the blues. Native to China.

Buddleia alternifolia (fountain buddleia) is hardy to zone 6, where it does not exhibit the dieback of *B. davidii*. It is also much more graceful and refined, its arching sprays of lilac-like flowers appearing in mid-May to June on the previous year's wood. Native to northwestern China.

Buxus sempervirens

Common boxwood
Zones 6 to 10
Broad-leafed evergreen

This is the most commonly used plant for topiary and trimmed hedges in formal gardens. The common boxwood also makes a good specimen in old age, since it grows quite slowly into a gnarled, spreading, and open treelike shrub, 10 to 20 feet in height and width. As a young plant it has a delicate, rounded, compact

habit. Its usefulness is limited to warm, moist climates without extremes of heat and cold, and it is subject to a wide variety of insect and disease pests. Plant boxwood in a well-drained, moist soil that has been generously amended with organic matter, and mulch heavily to provide a cool, moist root run. Annually prune out the inner dead twigs and remove the fallen leaves that accumulate in the branch crotches to prevent twig canker disease, common in the East. Never cultivate around boxwoods, because they root close to the surface. They do not tolerate drought. Protect them from drying winds and extreme emperatures, and give them partial shade in hot climates, full sun or partial shade elsewhere. Many cultivars are available for increased hardiness and in different forms and sizes. 'Northern Find' and 'Vardar Valley' are two of the hardiest (zone 5). Native to southern Europe, northern Africa, and western Asia.

Buxus microphylla (littleleaf boxwood, zones 6 to 10) Similar to the common boxwood, except that it is slightly hardier and more finely textured. Its foliage usually turns yellow-brown in cold weather. 'Tide Hill', 'Wintergreen', and other cultivars of *Buxus microphylla* var. *koreana* (Korean boxwood) are hardy to zone 5 and retain excellent green foliage all winter long. Other cultivars include 'Morris Midget', 'Morris Dwarf', and 'Kingsville Dwarf'. Cultural instructions and landscape uses are the same as for the common boxwood. Native to Japan.

Callistemon citrinus

Lemon bottlebrush, crimson bottlebrush
Zones 9 to 10
Broad-leafed evergreen

Common in the gardens of southern California and Florida, this evergreen, drought-tolerant plant displays bright red, brushlike flowers—effective in the landscape and attractive to hummingbirds—throughout most of the year. It

has fragrant, lemon-scented leaves. A massive shrub, growing 10 to 15 feet in height and width into a roundheaded, open form, the lemon bottlebrush is best used as a screen, a tall, informal hedge, or a specimen. It is excellent for the desert landscape as it tolerates drought and a wide range of soils, including those that are alkaline and saline. Both good drainage and full sun are preferred. Select named varieties from your nursery, because this plant is quite undependable when grown from seed. Cultivars vary in flower color, flower size, and compactness. Native to Australia.

Calluna vulgaris

Scotch heather
Zones 5 to 7
Narrow-leafed evergreen

Although its finely textured evergreen foliage, delicate colorful flowers, and low restrained habit make this one of the most treasured ground covers or rock garden plants, Scotch heather can be a difficult plant to grow. It must

Calycanthus floridus (Carolina allspice, strawberry-shrub)

Camellia japonica 'Kramer's Supreme' (camellia)

have perfectly drained soil that also retains moisture well. The best soil is acid (pH 6 or less), sandy or highly organic, and infertile. Too rich a soil causes heather to stretch and decrease flower production. Best in full sun, it does well in partial shade but flowers less. Mulch well and do not cultivate around the shallow roots. Heather does not tolerate drought. Prune or shear each fall after flowering to maintain compactness and encourage heavier blooming. Many cultivars are available for size variation (4 to 24 inches high by 2 feet or more wide), flower color (whites, pinks, purples), time of bloom (midsummer to fall), and foliage color (deep green to yellow or bronze). Native to Europe and Asia Minor.

Calycanthus floridus

Carolina allspice,
strawberry-shrub
Zones 5 to 9
Deciduous

A fragrant, easy-to-care-for shrub. Plant it near outdoor living areas, under windows, beside screen doors, in shrub borders, or wherever else the fragrance will be appreciated. The 2-inch, reddish brown flowers are quite dull in appearance. Flowers provide a sweet, strawberry scent in mid-May, and often sporadically into July. The shrub grows slowly to a neat, rounded outline, 6 to 9 feet high and 6 to 12 feet wide. It grows in nearly any soil, but performs best in deep, moist loam. Although adaptable to sun or shade, it does not grow as tall in full sun. The shrub transplants readily and is highly resistant to pests. Prune after flowering. Native to the moist woods from Virginia to Florida. *Calycanthus fertilis,* another eastern native occasionally mistaken for Carolina allspice, and *C. occidentalis,* a western native, are similar species, but neither has the pleasing floral fragrance of the Carolina allspice. Since fragrance is the chief motive for acquiring *Calycanthus floridus,* purchase it while it is in flower to ensure positive identification.

Camellia japonica

Common camellia
Zones 8 to 10
Broad-leafed evergreen

A favorite in southern gardens for its large, beautiful flowers in winter and early spring and its dense, polished, dark evergreen foliage, the camellia makes a fine specimen alone or in a mixed shrub border. It is especially effective when massed or in groups in shady gardens, and blends with other broad-leafed evergreens.

Although its size can vary according to cultivars, a height of 6 to 12 feet is common; occasionally in great age it can reach 20 feet or so. Often single trunked and branching well up from the ground, the effect is usually a roundish, densely foliaged mass that is nearly as broad as it is tall. The flowers are extremely variable—there are over three thousand named varieties—and normally last for about a month. The blooming season differs according to cultivar, from early (October to January) to mid-season (January to March) to late (March to May). The form of the flower varies from single to double with various degrees of flutes and frills. The colors range from white to red, and the size ranges from 2½ inches to 5 inches in diameter.

Camellias are often grouped with rhododendrons for cultural requirements, but this is not quite accurate. Camellias are not as particular about soil, and withstand heavy soils better than rhododendrons, but they still need organic matter and slight acidity (pH 6). Avoid overfertilization and salt buildup in the soil, and give them average watering. Avoid cultivating around their shallow roots.

Many varieties set too many flower buds. If large blossoms are sought, disbud in midsummer by removing all but two flower buds on each branch end, and one for every 2 to 4 inches of branch along the stems—the flower buds are fat and round; the leaf buds are slender.

Petal blight is a serious, disfiguring disease that causes petals to turn an ugly brown.

Caragana arborescens 'Lorbergii' (Siberian peashrub)

Caryopteris × *clandonensis* 'Longwood Blue' (blue spirea, bluebeard)

Ceanothus species (wild lilac)

Sanitation is the best control. Remove fallen petals and dispose of and replace the mulch every year. Native to China and Japan.

Camellia sasanqua (Sasanqua camellia, zones 7B to 10)   This is similar to the common camellia, except that it blooms earlier, from autumn to early winter. Again, tremendous variety is available for flower and form. Some are low-growing, sprawling shrubs that are useful for ground covers and espaliers; others make good hedges or screens. Very resistant to full sun. All make good specimens. Native to China and Japan.

Caragana arborescens

Siberian peashrub
Zones 2 to 7
Deciduous

Valuable for a hedge, screen, or windbreak where growing conditions are difficult—especially in the northern plains states—the Siberian peashrub contributes bright yellow flowers to the early to mid-May

landscape. A large shrub, growing rapidly into a sparse, angular and open structure 15 feet high and 12 feet wide, it is often trained as a small tree. Shearing encourages denser growth, but it is not suited for neat, formal hedges. The Siberian peashrub resists most pests, although leafhoppers can be damaging. It grows well in dry, rocky soils and exposed, windy sites, making it an effective answer to a difficult spot. 'Nana', a dwarf form with contorted branches, and 'Pendula', with angular, weeping branches grafted to a standard, are two interesting cultivars. Native to Siberia, Manchuria, and Mongolia.

Caryopteris × clandonensis

Blue spirea, bluebeard
Zones 6 to 8
Deciduous

Valuable for a subtle, unusual, blue haze of flowers from mid-August to frost, the blue spirea is most striking when contrasted against white or yellow flowers or massed in large

groups. Otherwise, its gray-blue, misty effect can easily get lost in the landscape. The blue spirea usually dies back to the ground each winter, growing each year to a loose, open, airy 2- to 3-foot shrub. In milder climates where it does not die back, it becomes a gangly, floppy, unattractive shrub. Plant blue spirea as a perennial in the border, cutting it back to the ground each winter to keep it compact and to increase the blooms. Give it average water and good garden soil. 'Azure' has bright blue flowers, as does 'Heavenly Blue', although it is slightly more tender. 'Blue Mist' has light blue flowers.

Ceanothus species

Wild lilac
Zones 8 to 10 (in the West)
Both broad-leafed evergreen and deciduous species

This genus of shrubs is generally most useful in West Coast gardens, where over forty species can be grown. Two deciduous species, *Ceanothus americanus* and *C. ovatus*, are native to eastern

North America, but the western evergreen natives are the ones that have the most ornamental interest. *Ceanothus* has beautiful, fragrant blue or white flowers and usually glossy, dark evergreen leaves.

Many species and varieties are available, from 8-inch ground covers to 30-foot small trees. The evergreen varieties are intolerant of heavy soils and too much water. Plant them in very rocky, sandy soil and away from sprinklers. Except for the initial season or two of establishment, they require little water. Plant wild lilac only in full sun. Prune only during the dry summer months to avoid transmitting a deadly canker disease. These shrubs are effective in large masses, either as ground covers on large, rocky slopes, or as higher, billowing masses. Occasionally, they are used as specimens for the striking blue flowers of some cultivars. *Ceanothus* becomes rangy with age, and most live for a relatively short time. Check with your nursery for the species or cultivar most useful to you.

Chaenomeles speciosa (common flowering quince)

Chamaecyparis thyoides (white cedar)

Chaenomeles speciosa

Common flowering quince
Zones 5 to 9
Deciduous

Although this shrub is the most ornamental of the quinces, its only assets are early spring flowers that are showy for about 10 days and a thorniness that is good for barriers. For the rest of the year it is less attractive. Variable in habit, it is usually a rounded, dense shrub 6 to 10 feet high and as wide, but cultivars are available from prostrate to open to erect forms, some of which are thornless. The plant tends to collect trash and is unsightly in exposed winter branches.

Quince flowers in late March (late February in the South) and is available in a wide array of very similar cultivars, from red and scarlet to pink and white. The fragrant fruit makes good jams and jellies. Common flowering quince is easy to grow and adaptable to a wide variety of conditions and soils, including dry soils and prairie drought. This quince flowers most when placed in full sun and pruned annually after spring bloom to about 6 inches from the ground. Leaf spots—particularly in wet climates—and scale can be problems, as well as chlorosis in alkaline soils. It does not flower as prolifically in warm-winter climates. Native to China.

Chamaecyparis species

False-cypress
Zones 4 to 8 (depending upon species)
Conifer

In this genus composed of large trees, a variety of dwarf cultivars are available that can be used as coniferous evergreen shrubs. Many species adapt to moderate and moist coastal climates, and a few perform well in the harsher conditions of the Midwest. With evergreen foliage similar to the juvenile leaves of junipers, cultivars vary according to foliage color—bright yellows, deep greens, grays, and blues—and habit—from small tufts to open, picturesque small trees. Transplant false-cypress into rich, well-drained soil in the spring, and give it full sun in moist, mild climates and partial shade elsewhere. Most *Chamaecyparis* die out in the center and lose lower branches with age—a strong jet of water is the easiest way to remove this foliage. Protect all *Chamaecyparis* from hot, drying winds.

Chamaecyparis lawsoniana (Lawson false-cypress, zones 6 to 8)   The best adapted to coastal, moist climates, this false-cypress is not suitable for midwestern conditions. Root rot is a significant problem on the West Coast. Yellow-leafed varieties are susceptible to burn from hot sun and drying winds. Native to southwestern Oregon and northwestern California.

Chamaecyparis obtusa (Hinoki false-cypress, zones 5 to 8)   Tolerating neutral soils somewhat better than other false-cypresses, this is the best choice for midwestern conditions. It is available in a wide variety of dwarf forms. Native to Japan and Formosa.

Chamaecyparis pisifera (Sawara false-cypress, zones 4 to 8)   The hardiest of the false-cypresses, this one loses its inner and lower foliage with age, and prefers acid soil. Native to Japan.

Choisya ternata

Mexican-orange
Zones 8B to 10
Broad-leafed evergreen

The early, deliciously scented white flowers of this shrub are a delight near entryways, outdoor living areas, windows, walkways, and paths—wherever fragrance can be enjoyed. The evergreen, fan-shaped foliage is produced densely at the ends of branches, creating an interesting layered, sculptured texture that is effective as an informal hedge or screen. The Mexican-orange is sensitive to soil conditions, needing well-drained acid soil that is rich in organic matter, and is intolerant of alkaline or high-salt soils. It tolerates full sun on the coast but needs partial shade in hot-summer climates. In too deep shade it becomes leggy and straggly

Choisya ternata (Mexican-orange)

Clethra alnifolia (summersweet, sweet pepperbush)

Cistus × *purpureus* (rockrose)

Cornus alba 'Sibirica' (Siberian dogwood)

and is prone to insect attacks. Water infrequently but deeply, and prune yearly to maintain a compact, dense form about 4 to 5 feet high and wide. Native to Mexico.

Cistus species

Rockrose
Zones 8 to 10
Broad-leafed evergreen

Useful in the Mediterranean-like climates of the West, rockroses make a colorful, low-maintenance, large-scale bank and ground cover. The foliage is fragrant, especially on hot days. Drought resistant and adaptable to salt spray, ocean winds, and desert heat, rockroses are bushy, dense, rounded shrubs that generally grow 3 to 4 feet tall and 4 to 5 feet wide. When massed they give the effect of a billowing dark or gray-green sea of foliage. Give them fast-draining soil, and pinch the tips of young plants to encourage denser growth. Do not move them once established as they do not transplant well. Native to the Mediterranean region.

Clethra alnifolia

Summersweet, sweet pepperbush
Zones 3 to 9
Deciduous

In addition to bearing fragrant, white spikes that bloom in July and August, summersweet is useful in wet, shady areas of the garden, although it thrives in nearly any soil. Once established, it grows slowly to a broad, oval mass 3 to 8 feet high and 4 to 8 feet wide. Its dark green, pest-free foliage turns a clear yellow in the fall before dropping.

Although tolerant of salty, sandy coastal conditions, it does best in moist, acid soil that is supplemented with organic matter. Plant in early spring and water profusely. Though native to swamps, nursery-grown *Clethra* is usually grown in well-drained soils, so the roots are no longer adapted to swampy soil conditions. When transplanting into wet soils, ease the transition by planting 3 to 4 inches higher than the soil level and by mulching. Pruning should be done in early spring. Allow

the shrub to attain its naturally dense, oval shape. *Clethra* is intolerant of drought, and it attracts bees while in flower. 'Paniculata', a cultivar with longer flowered spikes, is superior to the typical species. 'Rosea' has pink buds that open into flowers of white tinged with pink. Native to swamps and moist, sandy soils from Maine to Florida.

Coprosma repens

Mirrorplant
Zones 9 to 10
Broad-leafed evergreen

When pruned to restrain its rapid, sometimes awkward upright growth to 10 feet high and 6 feet wide, the extremely shiny, glossy leaves of this plant make it an excellent, quickly forming hedge, screen, foundation plant, or espalier. Because the flowers and fruits are inconspicuous, and its habit is rangy and open when neglected, use this shrub for its attractive evergreen foliage where you don't mind occasionally having to train it. Mirrorplant adapts well to

seashore conditions and is drought tolerant once established. Give it full sun on the coast or partial shade in hot inland areas. It does well in nearly any soil, grows rapidly, and needs regular pruning to keep it dense and neat. Several forms have yellow or white variegated leaves. *Coprosma* × *kirkii* is a wide-spreading, 2- to 3-foot-high shrub that makes a tough evergreen ground cover, particularly where erosion may be a problem. Native to New Zealand.

Cornus alba 'Sibirica'

Siberian dogwood
Zones 2 to 8
Deciduous

The bright red winter stems of this dogwood distinguish it from all other landscape plants, and it can be difficult to integrate into the garden. Its loose, open, and very erect branches grow rapidly to a height of 8 to 10 feet, with lateral branching occurring only in the upper third of the

Corylus avellana 'Contorta' (Harry Lauder's walkingstick)

Cotinus coggygria (smoke tree)

shrub. The spread is variable, ranging from 5 to 10 feet. Extremely vigorous and apt to overgrow neighboring shrubs, the Siberian dogwood is also difficult to use as a single specimen. It can be effective in the shrub border, however, and is especially beautiful when massed on a large scale, such as along drives, on banks, or naturalized around a pond. Siberian dogwood transplants easily and is adaptable to nearly any soil when it has sun or light shade. Like most dogwoods, it is susceptible to many pests and diseases. Maintaining a vigorous plant is the best protection. In order to encourage vigorous new growth with bright winter stem color, each spring remove at least one third of the old wood—more if a compact plant is desired. Native from Siberia to Manchuria and North Korea.

Cornus sericea, also listed as *C. stolonifera* (redosier dogwood, zones 2 to 8)   This is the North American counterpart to *Cornus alba,* differing chiefly in its more muted, dark red winter stem color, and its preference for moist, waterlogged soils. *C. sericea* 'Flaviramea' has an unusual bright yellow winter stem color, but is highly susceptible to cankers and twig blights. These are generally not a problem, however, if the shrub is pruned heavily each spring. Dwarf forms, such as 'Isanti', have recently appeared on the market. Native to wet places from Newfoundland to Manitoba and south to Virginia and Nebraska.

Corylus avellana 'Contorta'

Harry Lauder's walkingstick, corkscrew hazel

Zone 5
Deciduous

A distinctive shrub with uniquely curled and twisted stems, twigs, and leaves that impart a decidedly Asian flavor, Harry Lauder's walkingstick is best used as an accent or focal point in an entryway or courtyard. It is especially effective against a light-colored wall because of its interesting winter silhouette. A rapid grower, it forms a rounded mass of contorted, snaking branches 8 to 10 feet in height and width, and can even become a 20-foot small tree. The flowers are pendulous yellowish or tan catkins that are quite unusual and showy in March before the leaves appear. Adaptable to a wide range of soils, acidity, and sunlight, it is an easy plant to grow. Select plants in the nursery that are propagated by cuttings, and thus are growing on their own roots. For grafted plants, immediately prune out any suckers that arise from below the graft union because the more vigorous understock has a tendency to overtake the contorted top growth.

Cotinus coggygria

Smoke tree

Zones 6 to 8 (grows in zones 4 and 5 with winter dieback)
Deciduous

A long-lasting, cloudlike pinkish or whitish display in midsummer, along with several good purple-leafed cultivars, have made this a favorite in the low-maintenance garden. Commonly growing to as high as 25 feet, the smoke tree is usually a loose, open shrub with many upright stems 10 to 15 feet in height and greater in width, creating a rounded and irregular appearance. Most useful for the shrub border as a textural and color accent, and in massings and groups, this is not good for single specimen use. The foliage on the species is an attractive blue-green with occasionally outstanding fall color in the reds, yellows, and purples.

Many of the purple-leafed cultivars fade to green as the season progresses. An exception is 'Velvet Cloak', which retains its purple color throughout the season. The floral display varies from pink to whitish and is only showy on predominantly female plants, so purchase only named varieties. 'Daydream' is an especially floriferous form with pink pedicels.

Cotoneaster dammeri (bearberry cotoneaster)

Cotoneaster horizontalis (rock cotoneaster)

The smoke tree is easily transplanted and adapts to a wide variety of soils, including dry, rocky ones. Give it full sun. It must have frequent and deep watering when young, but is drought tolerant once established. Prune only to remove dead branches as each pruning cut stimulates several long, slender shoots into growth, ultimately creating a ragged, unkempt-appearing plant. Another species, *Cotinus obovatus,* is a large shrub with excellent foliage. Native from southern Europe to central China.

Cotoneaster dammeri

Bearberry cotoneaster
Zones 6 to 9
Broad-leafed evergreen

The glossy, dense leaves, good fruiting color, rapid growth, and low, prostrate habit make this one of the best hardy, broad-leafed evergreens for ground covering. It can be used on banks and slopes, in masses, in a shrub border, or as a low facing plant for tall, leggy shrubs. The bearberry cotoneaster spreads rapidly to 6 feet or more wide, its branches rooting where they touch the ground, and remains under 1½ feet high. The finely textured, lustrous, dark green leaves are speckled with white flowers in late May, followed in late summer by bright red, berrylike pomes like tiny apples. Some cultivars, such as 'Coral Beauty', flower and fruit more freely than species plants. 'Lowfast' is hardier to southern zone 5. 'Strybing's Finding' has a low, prostrate habit. *C. dammeri* transplants easily from containers and is adaptable to many soils, although it prefers fast drainage. It is an excellent choice for dry, rocky soil in an exposed, sunny location. Fireblight and aphids can be problems. Native to central China.

Cotoneaster divaricatus

Spreading cotoneaster
Zones 5B to 9
Deciduous

This is one of the most handsome cotoneasters for summer and fall foliage, fruit, and graceful form. Use it in a shrub border where it blends well with other shrubs, and consider it for informal hedges, masses, and groupings as a refined textural asset. It rapidly grows to 5 to 6 feet high and 6 to 8 feet wide. Rose-colored flowers bloom in May, and bright to dark red fruits nearly cover the plant from September through November. The finely textured foliage is a dark, glossy green in summer, changing in the fall to brilliant fluorescent yellow and red combinations that remain for a long time as the shrub is one of the last to defoliate. Preferring well-drained, moist, and fertile soils, spreading cotoneaster nevertheless performs well in dry, rocky sites. The shrub is wind tolerant, adapts to various pH levels, and is a good choice for seashore conditions. Give it full sun or light shade. *C. divaricatus* is one of the most trouble-free of the cotoneasters. Native to western and central China.

Cotoneaster horizontalis

Rock cotoneaster
Zones 5B to 9
Deciduous (semievergreen in mild climates)

Spilling over walls, down slopes, and over rocks, the angular, layered form and herringbone branches of the rock cotoneaster add an unusual texture to the garden. Commonly used as a large-scale bank or ground cover for excellent erosion control, this 2- to 3-foot-high shrub spreads 5 to 8 feet or more. The attractive pink flowers can be abundant from late May to early June, attracting bees. Red berries dot the plants from late August through November and can be quite showy. The plant's glossy, semievergreen foliage is deciduous in northern areas, where it turns orange and red before dropping. In mild climates, the leaves usually remain a glossy green all winter. See *C. dammeri* for cultural suggestions. Many cultivars are available for differences in form and foliage color. Native to China.

Cotoneaster multiflorus (many-flowered cotoneaster)

Daphne cneorum (garlandflower)

Cotoneaster multiflorus

Many-flowered cotoneaster
Zones 6 to 9
Deciduous

One of the most trouble-free of the cotoneasters, this shrub is also one of the most beautiful. Its white early to mid-May flowers are followed by bright red berries that last from late August into October. In habit it is a graceful, arching, mounded, or fountainlike shrub that grows 8 to 12 or more feet high and 12 to 15 feet wide. In flower and form it is similar to, and a good substitute for, a large Vanhoutte spirea. It is definitely not a shrub for the small landscape—use it in a shrub border or for massing in spacious areas where it has plenty of room to grow. The foliage is blue-green with a medium-fine texture and has little or no coloration before dropping in the fall. Plant container-grown plants in well-drained soil in a sunny, airy location. Root-prune the plants as you set them out to help develop a strong, fibrous root system. Native to China.

Cytisus × praecox

Warminster broom
Zones 6 to 10
Deciduous (with evergreen stems)

Although not strictly evergreen, the Warminster broom has that effect due to its dense, vertical stems that remain green all winter long. Even in the summer, foliage is sparse or nonexistent; nearly all the photosynthesis takes place in the green stems, which in all seasons are the plant's main textural asset. In May, the addition of profuse, pale yellow flowers creates a showy display. Use this plant as a specimen in a shrub border, in large rock gardens where dry, poor soil presents a problem, or where an interesting textural evergreen accent in winter and a showy spring display are desired. Under most conditions this shrub grows 4 to 6 feet high with an equal or greater spread, for a rounded mass of many parallel, mostly vertical stems.

In spring, move young container-grown plants into well-drained soil. Bacteria on the roots of this plant fix nitrogen from the atmosphere, and it actually prefers infertile and poor soil. Young plants can be tip-pinched, but older plants do not respond well to pruning of any kind. Allow them to develop their natural form.

Many other *Cytisus* species are available, but most become rampant, naturalizing, self-sowing pests. Particularly notorious is Scotch broom (*C. scoparius*), which has caused much ecological damage on the West Coast and in parts of the Northeast. Unfortunately, it is one of the most commonly available brooms. Some cultivars, such as *C. scoparius* 'Carla', and most hybrids, such as *C. × praecox,* are generally not a weed problem. Native to the Mediterranean region.

Daphne cneorum

Garlandflower
Zones 5 to 7
Broad-leafed evergreen

This is one of the most fragrant shrubs available and has finely textured evergreen foliage with rosy-pink clusters of flowers at the ends of the branches in April and May. It grows slowly 6 to 12 inches high and 2 feet or more in spread, forming a low, loose trailing mass. Use it as a small-scale ground cover, in a rock garden, in shady spots, or in groupings where its fragrance can be most appreciated. Always plant daphne from containers into well-drained, moist, pH neutral soil. Protect the plants from hot sun and drying winds, mulch to keep the roots cool and moist, and don't disturb it after it is established by cultivating or trying to move it. Plant daphne fairly high to reduce the chances of crown rot. Native to central and southern Europe.

Daphne × burkwoodii (Burkwood daphne, zones 6 to 8)　A larger daphne with extremely fragrant flowers in May that open white and fade to pink, the Burkwood daphne grows compact and 3 to 4 feet high and wide. 'Somerset' is a larger cultivar, growing 4 to 5 feet wide, and is one of the easiest daphnes to grow. 'Carol Mackie' has variegated leaves.

Deutzia gracilis (slender deutzia)

Elaeagnus pungens (silverberry)

Daphne odora (winter daphne, zones 8 to 10)   More than any other, this daphne is responsible for the reputation of being unpredictable and frustrating—full-grown plants may suddenly die for no apparent reason. Despite this, it is the most popular daphne in mild regions, particularly for its wonderful fragrance. Rosy pink flowers that bloom in February and March adorn the lustrous, dark green, 3-inch-long leaves. This daphne must have perfect drainage and be planted high. Water infrequently during the summer months to increase flowering and prevent root rot. 'Marginata' is a hardier, easier-to-grow variegated form. Native to Japan and China.

Deutzia gracilis

Slender deutzia
Zones 5 to 8
Deciduous

Deutzia is another of the traditional, popular favorites that are showy for a short time in the spring. There are many deutzia species and cultivars, but this one is probably the most graceful in form and dependable for flower. A low, broad-mounded shrub 2 to 6 feet high and 3 to 6 feet wide with gracefully upright arching branches and dull green foliage, deutzia is best used in a shrub border where its plain appearance when not in flower can blend with other shrubs. In mid- to late May, pure white flowers cover the shrub. Easy to grow, *Deutzia gracilis* transplants readily in the spring into any reasonably good garden soil and takes full sun to light shade. Subject to severe winter dieback, deutzia should be pruned out annually. Deutzia flowers on old wood, so prune immediately after flowering. 'Nitto' is an excellent dwarf cultivar that reaches 12–18 inches high and 2–3 feet wide. Native to Japan.
   Deutzia × rosea 'Carminea' is more dwarf in habit, with a great abundance of rosy-pink flowers. *D. × lemoinei* is a twiggy, erect shrub 5 to 7 feet tall, with white flowers that appear after those of slender deutzia.

'Avalanche' is a more compact form that grows 4 feet high and wide.

Elaeagnus pungens

Silverberry
Zones 7 to 10
Broad-leafed evergreen

The plain but powerfully fragrant flowers that bloom in October and the evergreen, olive foliage are the distinguishing features of this hardy, adaptable shrub. It has thorny branches and edible red fruit in the spring. Good in problem areas of heat, wind, and drought, this shrub actually prefers poor, infertile soil, because it fixes its own nitrogen from the atmosphere. It responds well to shearing, which increases its density. This is an excellent hedge plant, and its thorny branches present an impenetrable barrier. Without pruning it rapidly becomes a rigid, sprawling, angular shrub growing from 6 to 15 feet tall. Cultivars are available for variegated foliage. Native to Japan.

Enkianthus campanulatus

Redvein enkianthus
Zones 5 to 9
Deciduous

Redvein enkianthus is a refined shrub with many ornamental features, including delicate, yellowish clusters of bell-like flowers in May that become veined with red, orange and red fall color, and an interesting horizontal branching structure. It is an excellent specimen plant and combines well with rhododendrons. Use it where it can be appreciated up close, such as around entryways or in outdoor living areas. A narrow, upright shrub or small tree with stratified branches and tufted foliage, it grows slowly 6 to 8 feet high in northern climates and can reach 20 to 30 feet in mild ones. Plant in moist, well-drained, acid soil that is rich in organic matter, in a location that has full sun to partial shade (shade is preferred in hot-summer climates). Does not tolerate drought or salts. Native to Japan.

Erica species (heath)

Escallonia × *langleyensis* 'Pride of Donard' (escallonia)

Erica species

Heath
Zones 4 to 8 (depending upon species)
Narrow-leafed evergreen

Similar to *Calluna* (heather), these evergreen shrubs have a more variable size, are generally more tender, and have an earlier spring bloom. The smaller forms make outstanding ground covers and masses, facing plants for a shrub border, and rock garden specimens. The larger forms make striking textural and color accents in the spring. All are most effective when grown in large masses or beds. Like heather, *Erica* can be difficult to grow (see *Calluna vulgaris,* page 67). Many of the species listed below have a large number of cultivars.

Erica arborea (tree heath, zones 9 to 10)   A rather awkward shrub or small tree that grows 10 to 20 feet high, its fragrant white flowers bloom from March to May.

Erica canaliculata (Christmas heath, zones 9 to 10)   A bushy shrub growing 6 to 8 feet tall with irregular spires

of foliage, this is often sold in containers around Christmas.

Erica carnea (spring heath, zones 6 to 8)   A dwarf, spreading form growing 6 to 16 inches high and 2 to 6 feet wide, this shrub tolerates more alkaline soils than most heaths. An annual pruning or shearing just after blooming gives heath its best look.

Erica mediterranea (Biscay or Mediterranean heath, zones 8 to 10)   With upright growth 4 to 7 feet high, this finely textured shrub is good strictly for background foliage, with plain flowers.

Erica vagans (Cornish heath, zones 6 to 8)   A bushy shrub that grows 2 to 3 feet tall and 3 to 4 feet wide, its flowers are the latest of the heaths to bloom—from July until September.

Escallonia rubra

Red escallonia
Zones 8 to 10
Broad-leafed evergreen

Fast growing, producing attractive red, fragrant flowers in the summer and fall

(year-around in milder climates), and tolerant of the wind and salt spray of coastal gardens, escallonia makes an excellent screen or windbreak and is useful for massing and integrating into the shrub border. Its dark, evergreen foliage responds well to pruning, although with a corresponding reduction in blooming. A light annual pruning maintains a compact form, but left to itself it quickly grows to 6 to 15 feet tall with a dense, rounded, and upright habit. Does not tolerate highly alkaline soils, and it needs partial shade in hot inland gardens. Tolerates short periods of drought, but performs best with adequate water. Native to South America.

Escallonia × *exoniensis* 'Balfourii' (zones 9 to 10) This escallonia grows as high as 10 feet, with graceful, drooping branchlets and pink blossoms.

Escallonia × *exoniensis* 'Frades' (zones 9 to 10) This hybrid produces more abundant pink flowers and retains a more compact 5- to 6-foot habit.

Euonymus alata

Burning-bush, winged euonymus
Zones 4 to 7
Deciduous

Popular especially for its brilliant scarlet fall color, *Euonymus alata* displays a neat, vase-shaped habit and clean, pest-free foliage. It eventually gets quite large and open—15 to 20 feet high and as wide—however, and this should be considered before it is used. Burning-bush is easily transplanted and adaptable to many soils and growing conditions, except to very wet ones. Pruning destroys the naturally neat outline of the plant, causing "witches' brooms" and uneven growth. It adapts equally well to full sun or heavy shade, where it still develops good fall color, although its brightest hues are in full sun. Use it as an unclipped hedge or screen, in groups, in the shrub border, or as a specimen. The cultivar 'Compactus' is a slightly smaller form, growing 10 to 15 feet in height and spread. It is often sold as an attractive small dwarf, which it most

Euonymus fortunei 'Green and Gold' (winter-creeper)

Exochorda racemosa (pearlbush)

Forsythia × *intermedia* (border forsythia)

certainly is not. 'Rudy Haag' and 'Nana' grow to 4–6 feet. 'Tetra Gold' is compact and upright, with a spreading habit. Native from northeastern Asia to central China.

Euonymus fortunei

Winter-creeper
Zones 5 to 8
Broad-leafed evergreen

Although it is popular as one of the hardiest broad-leafed evergreens, the shrub forms of winter-creeper should be used with caution due to their susceptibility to several serious diseases and insects. Many of the *Euonymus fortunei* cultivars are spreading, semiprostrate ground covers. The shrub forms are variable in habit and size. Some cultivars, propagated from juvenile growth, do not fruit; others bear heavy crops of bright orange fruit in fall and winter. Euonymus transplants easily, is tolerant of all but the wettest soils, and withstands full sun to heavy shade. In harsh, exposed locations, the foliage is prone to yellowing and browning in winter.

In moist, humid climates and sites with poor air circulation, mildew is a serious problem. Anthracnose, crown gall, and scale are even more serious, often killing entire plantings. Leaf spots, aphids, and thrips are also problems. Native to China.

Euonymus japonica (evergreen euonymus, Japanese spindle tree; zones 8 to 10)   A shrub or small tree that grows to a 15-foot width and an 8-foot spread, this is a low-maintenance, tough plant for harsh situations and poor soils. Susceptible to mildew and sucking insects—especially scale, aphids, mites, and thrips—plant where air circulation is good and where water does not stand. Many cultivars are available, the more popular being the strongly variegated golden and white forms.

Euonymus kiautschovica (spreading euonymus, zones 6 to 9)   This is generally an evergreen shrub growing 8 to 10 feet high, but in areas that have cold winters the foliage often turns yellow-brown and remains well into the winter.

It has the same pest problems as *E. fortunei*. 'Dupont' is a hardier, more compact form. 'Manhattan' is similar to 'Dupont'. 'Sieboldiana' has cleaner foliage and is more resistant to scale.

Exochorda racemosa

Pearlbush
Zones 5 to 8
Deciduous

Popular for its white buds that open into bloom in mid-May, this plant has little value the rest of the year. Pearlbush grows 9 to 15 feet in height and spread. This upright, irregular shrub becomes unruly as it gets older. Pruning the shrub annually just after flowering helps maintain a more compact habit. Plant it in well-drained, acid soil, give it full sun to partial shade and average watering, and it will attract no serious pests. Native to eastern China.

Exochorda × *macrantha* 'The Bride' is a superior hybrid cultivar. It is lower growing and more compact, growing 3 to 4 feet in height and spread.

Forsythia × intermedia

Border forsythia
Zones 5 to 9
Deciduous

Spectacular pale to deep yellow flowers in late March or early April (February to March in mild climates) are this shrub's only attribute. An upright, arching, and vigorous shrub that constantly needs grooming, it rapidly grows 8 to 10 feet high and 10 to 12 feet wide. Plant forsythia in nearly any soil, but give it plenty of water and feeding. A location in full sun maximizes flowering. Prune forsythia annually, right after it completes flowering, by removing one third of the oldest canes. Give it plenty of room and allow it to grow in its natural form; do not shear. Older, overgrown plants can be renewed by cutting them almost entirely to the ground. Although the roots are reasonably hardy, the flower buds are often killed by late freezes as far south as mid-zone 6. Select flower-bud hardy varieties, such as 'Karl Sax' and the Farrand hybrids, and

Fothergilla major (large fothergilla)

Fuchsia × *hybrida* (common fuchsia)

plant in protected areas in northern zones. Many cultivars are available for growth habit and for quantity, color, and size of bloom, ranging from pale to deep yellow.

Forsythia ovata (zone 4B) Although ornamentally inferior, this forsythia is useful in those northern, borderline areas where the flower buds of *Forsythia* × *intermedia* are often killed. Native to the mountains of Korea.

Forsythia suspensa (zones 5 to 8)   It is not as free-flowering as *Forsythia* × *intermedia,* but it displays a graceful, pendulous form excellent for cascading over banks and sides of streams. Native to China.

Fothergilla major

Large fothergilla
Zones 6 to 8
Deciduous

Fothergilla is one of the most attractive and desirable of the southeastern native shrubs. Its honey-scented, profuse white blooms resemble small, round bottlebrushes and flower in late April to early May. The clean, dark green, and pest-free foliage consistently provides a showy fall display of bright yellow, orange, and scarlet. It is a neat, rounded shrub that grows 6 to 10 feet high with a slightly narrower spread. Use fothergilla in groups, masses, and foundation planting. It is especially attractive as a specimen or integrated into the shrub border. Although an acid, well-drained soil is necessary, fothergilla is a relatively adaptable plant that is entirely pest-free. It grows well in partial shade and dry, rocky soils, but full sun and soils rich in organic matter improve the flowers and fall color. Native to dry, sunny ridges in the southern Appalachians from Virginia to South Carolina.

Fothergilla gardenii (dwarf fothergilla, zones 6 to 8) Differing from the large fothergilla in smaller size (to 3 feet) and flowers that bear before the leaves, this is an excellent shrub for small spaces. Rarely available in nurseries.

Fuchsia × hybrida

Common fuchsia
Zone 10
Deciduous to evergreen

Fuchsias are common evergreen (in frost-free areas), deciduous, or perennial shrubs in zone 10, and are often seen as houseplants elsewhere. Fuchsias are a widely variable group of plants that display bright, multicolored flowers and have a trailing to upright habit. Blooming from early summer until frost, the flowers attract hummingbirds. Some forms make excellent trailing cascades for hanging baskets or stream banks; others can be used as upright specimens or integrated into the shrub border, and are often espaliered.

Fuchsias definitely perform best in areas with cool summers, high atmospheric moisture, filtered shade, and moist, rich soil high in organic matter. In dry climates especially, they should be mulched heavily, misted and watered frequently, and protected from hot, searing winds. Give them light applications of liquid fertilizer every 10 to 14 days throughout the growing season, spray regularly to control sucking insects, and pinch them back frequently to encourage dense growth. Prune annually in the early spring before new growth starts by removing about the same amount of wood as was formed the previous season. Always leave at least two healthy buds on each branch.

Fuchsia magellanica (hardy fuchsia, zones 6 to 10)   In northern areas this shrub is a perennial, dying to the ground and growing to a rounded 3-foot shrub each year. In the Deep South it commonly reaches 4 to 8 feet high. The flowers are bright red with blue inner petals, and are smaller than those of the common fuchsia. They bear profusely from late June until frost. A graceful shrub with attractive foliage, it performs best in partial shade and rich, well-drained but moist soil (although it is not as demanding as *Fuchsia* × *hybrida*). Native to Chile.

Gardenia jasminoides (gardenia)

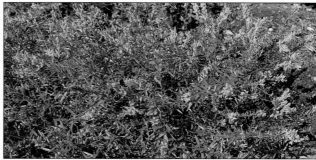

Genista tinctoria (common woadwaxen)

Hamamelis × intermedia (hybrid witchhazel)

Gardenia jasminoides

Gardenia
Zones 8 to 10
Broad-leafed evergreen

The fragrance of gardenia flowers and the glossy, evergreen leaves are an asset to any garden. Use gardenias as specimens in containers and raised beds, as hedges and low screens, or as espaliers. Most varieties grow 3 to 6 feet high and wide. Lower growing forms, such as 'Radicans', make effective ground covers on a limited scale.

Gardenias do not tolerate alkaline soil, saline water, poor drainage, or drought. Plant their crowns high in an acid soil rich in organic matter. They prefer a protected location of partial shade, full sun in foggy areas. Late frosts can be damaging, especially at the northern limits of their range. Mist the foliage regularly in the early mornings while the plant is not in bloom, and feed every 3 to 4 weeks during the growing season with an acid plant food. Spray regularly to control sucking insects. Gardenias do not bloom well in cool-summer areas. 'Radicans Variegata' has a pale yellow margin and does best in zones 9 and 10. Native to China.

Genista tinctoria

Common woadwaxen
Zones 2 to 9
Deciduous

This is the hardiest of the *Genista* species and features yellow flowers in June and a small, rounded habit that is 2 to 3 feet high, composed of vertical, nearly leafless, evergreen stems. All *Genista* species require full sun and quick drainage, but beyond that are easy to grow and adaptable, preferring poor, dry, infertile soil. They tolerate drought and coastal conditions well. Leave genistas alone after they become established—they do not move easily. All *Genista* species are native to the Mediterranean region.

Genista hispanica (Spanish gorse or Spanish broom, zones 6B to 9) This shrub has bright yellow flowers in early June, grows 1 to 2 feet high, and spreads quite wide.

Genista monosperma (bridalveil broom, zones 9 to 10) This shrub bears white, fragrant flowers in both winter and spring. It is a large, upright shrub, growing 20 feet high and 10 feet wide.

Genista pilosa (silkyleaf woadwaxen, zones 6 to 10) Bearing yellow flowers in late May, this shrub grows 1 to 1½ feet tall and 7 feet wide. It has silvery leaves.

Genista sagittalis (arrow broom, zones 5 to 10) This rapidly growing prostrate shrub has outstanding yellow flowers in May and June. It grows 6 to 12 inches high and 7 feet wide.

Hamamelis × intermedia

Hybrid witchhazel
Zones 6 to 8
Deciduous

Witchhazels have spicy, fragrant, delicately showy winter flowers. During periods of extreme cold, the flower petals curl up into a tight ball, and thus can withstand prolonged periods of being covered with ice in 0° F weather. Although this hybrid is not as fragrant or restrained in size as others, it is the showiest of all witchhazels available in the United States. As early as February its leafless branches are covered with deep yellow blossoms that last about a month. The red-flowered cultivars, such as 'Jelena', are not as outstanding from a distance as the ones with yellow flowers. This is not a shrub for small gardens as it eventually reaches 15 to 20 feet in height with a comparable spread. Leaves turn vivid reds, oranges, and yellows before dropping.

Plant witchhazels in deep, rich soils that have an abundant supply of moisture. Although they do not tolerate drought, they are virtually pest-free. Use them as screens, backgrounds, or large focal points, or train them into small trees. They make an excellent choice for a naturalized woodland understory and for planting near windows, where they can be seen from indoors in winter.

Hibiscus syriacus (shrub-althea, rose-of-Sharon)

Hydrangea macrophylla 'Blue Wave' (bigleaf hydrangea)

Hamamelis vernalis (vernal witchhazel, zones 6 to 9) With powerfully fragrant, small, yellow flowers in January and February, this witchhazel has a neater, smaller habit (6 to 10 feet high and usually much wider) that is round and dense. The leaves turn a clear yellow in the fall. Native to gravelly, often-flooded stream banks in the Ozark Mountains.

Hamamelis virginiana (common witchhazel, zones 5 to 9) This is the hardiest but also the largest and rangiest of the witchhazels, growing 20 to 30 feet high and wide. Its yellow flowers in November and December often coincide with clear yellow fall foliage, reducing their effectiveness, but they are quite fragrant. Native to forests from Canada to Georgia and west to Nebraska.

Hibiscus syriacus

Shrub-althea, rose-of-Sharon
Zones 6 to 9
Deciduous

A traditional favorite for its late-summer-to-frost flowers. The shrub-althea is most

effective when grouped or massed in a shrub border. It is a large, very erect and round-topped shrub or small tree that grows, at a medium rate, 8 to 12 feet tall and 6 to 10 feet wide. A large variety of cultivars is available for flower color—whites, reds, purples, violets, and various combinations. It is tolerant of the salt and wind of coastal gardens and prefers a hot summer. Wet weather tends to rot the flower buds. Although not particular about soils, the shrub-althea does not do well in wet or dry ones. Best in full sun, it tolerates partial shade. If left unpruned, the flowers are profuse but small. For larger flowers, prune hard each spring—it flowers on the current year's growth—to two to three buds per stem. Its leaves are among the last to appear in the spring and the first to drop in the fall. Spray regularly for Japanese beetles, scale, aphids, and whiteflies. This shrub is susceptible to a wide range of diseases in humid climates. 'Diana' has a clear, white flower. 'Blue bird' is light blue. Native to China and India.

Hibiscus rosa-sinensis (Chinese hibiscus, zones 9 to 10) Popular in Florida, California, Texas, and Hawaii, this shrub grows rapidly to 30 feet high. Thousands of cultivars are available, with large, platelike flowers. Hibiscus requires good drainage, abundant moisture, sun, and heat, and protection from wind and frost. It seldom blooms in cool-summer areas. Feed it monthly during the growing season and protect it from aphids. Prune out about one third of the old wood each spring to keep older plants vigorous and tip-pinch to increase bloom. Native to China.

Hydrangea macrophylla

Bigleaf hydrangea, French hydrangea
Zones 7 to 10
Deciduous

This hydrangea has a good late-summer floral display (July to August) and lustrous, neat foliage in mild-winter areas. It is also commonly grown in pots by florists. Varieties suitable as container

plants are not as satisfactory in the garden. When grown outside, it is a round shrub with many erect, infrequently branched stems reaching 4 to 8 feet in height (sometimes 12 feet) and widely spreading, due to its tendency to sucker vigorously. Many cultivars are available, and are generally divided between the hortensias, with all-sterile flowers forming large globular heads, and the lace-caps, which have a delicate ring of large sterile flowers surrounding a cluster of tiny fertile ones. Flowers can be single or double, are available in white, pinks, and blues, and are generally clustered in heads that are 5 to 10 inches in diameter. The bigleaf hydrangea prefers seashore conditions, where it can be planted in full sun. Otherwise, plant it in partial shade and in moist, rich, well-drained soil high in organic matter. The acidity of the soil affects the uptake of aluminum by the plant, which in turn determines whether the flowers are pink or blue. Blue flowers result from a pH of 5 to 5.5, and pink flowers occur

Hydrangea quercifolia (oakleaf hydrangea)

Iberis sempervirens (evergreen candytuft)

in soils with a pH of 6 to 6.5 or higher. Apply aluminum sulfate to the soil to increase acidity and provide aluminum for blue flowers; apply lime to decrease the acidity for pink flowers. Apply well before blooming to achieve the color desired. Bigleaf hydrangeas flower on old wood, so pruning should be done just after flowering. Native to Japan.

Hydrangea quercifolia

Oakleaf hydrangea
Zones 6 to 9
Deciduous

The lacy, delicate white flowers and deep red or purplish fall leaves make this an attractive shrub; the foliage texture is often the chief feature in the garden. Its attractively coarse, clean foliage is useful in the shrub border for an accent in large masses, in difficult shady places, or as a specimen. An upright and irregular shrub that grows slowly, 6 to 8 feet high and 4 to 6 feet wide, it has a tendency to sucker from the roots and form large colonies. The

conical flower clusters appear in late June through July and are white and lacy, the large sterile flowers surrounding the tiny fertile ones in a ring. The flowers persist on the shrub for a long time, fading to pink, then to purplish pink, and finally to brown. Plant it in moist, fertile, well-drained soil on the acid side, in sun or half shade. If necessary, it tolerates dense shade quite well, although the fall leaf color is less and fewer flowers are produced. Mulch well in dry climates to maintain a cool, moist root run. Because this shrub flowers on old wood, it is strictly a foliage plant where winters reach 0° F or colder; severe weather causes serious dieback. Native to Georgia and Florida, west to Mississippi.

Hypericum prolificum

Shrubby St.-Johnswort
Zones 5 to 9
Deciduous

The bright yellow flowers of this hardiest *Hypericum* bloom from mid-June through

August. Fresh, clean, blue-green foliage covers this dense, rounded shrub that grows 1 to 4 feet high and wide. Suited to bright sun and well-drained, light soil, *H. prolificum* is tough, pest-resistant, and easy to maintain. It tolerates poor, dry, sterile soil, city air pollution, and partial shade. Although seldom necessary, pruning should be done in late spring after new growth hardens off. Use shrubby St.-Johnswort in a border, for large-scale masses or small groupings, as foundation plantings, or as a low, informal hedge. Native from New Jersey to Iowa and Georgia.

Hypericum × moseranum (goldflower St.-Johnswort, zones 8 to 10) A low, evergreen shrub, this is one of the few plants that does well under eucalyptus trees.

Hypericum calycinum (Aaron's-beard, zones 6 to 10) A low-growing, deciduous shrub suitable for ground covering, it becomes weedy and difficult to control. Mow to the ground every few years as necessary.

Hypericum frondosum (golden St.-Johnswort, zones 6 to 9) This species grows 3 to 4 feet high and wide and has handsome, blue-green foliage and large, bright yellow flowers. 'Sunburst' is a lower-growing form (2 to 4 feet high and wide).

Hypericum patulum (goldencup St.-Johnswort, zones 7 to 10) This is a semi-evergreen or evergreen species growing as high and wide as 3 feet. Variety *henryi* is more vigorous and has larger flowers. 'Hidcote' is a smaller, 18-inch shrub with large, fragrant, yellow flowers that bloom from June to October. 'Sungold' is still more hardy.

Iberis sempervirens

Evergreen candytuft
Zones 5 to 10
Broad-leafed evergreen

A handsome, mat-forming evergreen shrub that produces generous drifts of pure white flowers in April or May, candytuft is useful as a ground cover interplanted with woody

Ilex cornuta 'Rotunda' (dwarf Chinese holly)

Ilex crenata 'Hetzii' (Japanese holly)

shrubs and in combination with spring bulbs. Extremely showy in bloom, the neat, 6- to 12-inch-high shrub spreads wide and is covered in all seasons by dark green, finely textured foliage. It transplants easily, either from containers or as seedlings, into light soil that has average fertility. Do not overfertilize or it becomes loose and rangy. Prune hard each year after flowering. Removal of spent flowers is important to increase next year's bloom and to keep plants dense. Give good drainage—excessive moisture encourages several severe disease problems. 'Christmas Snow' repeats its bloom in the fall. 'Little Gem' is more of a dwarf and hardier than the species. 'Purity' is similar, but has larger flower clusters. Native to southern Europe and western Asia.

Ilex cornuta

Chinese holly
Zones 7 to 10
Broad-leafed evergreen

Although the species is a large, upright shrub 10 to 15 feet tall, many smaller, denser cultivars of this shrub are available. The leaves are dark, polished green in all seasons, and are larger and coarser than Japanese holly. The fruits are a brilliant red and bear profusely. Unlike other hollies, the fruits develop without fertilization, so having both male and female plants is not necessary. 'Dwarf Burford', 'Carissa', and 'Dazzler' are heavy fruiting forms that have a slow-growing, dwarf habit. 'Rotunda' is especially dense and low growing. 'Burfordii' is a hardier cultivar that does well in zone 6. See *Ilex crenata* (Japanese holly) for cultural recommendations. Native to eastern China and Korea.

Ilex crenata

Japanese holly
Zones 6B to 10
Broad-leafed evergreen

This holly is commonly mistaken for boxwood because of its neat, rounded shape and dark green, dense, lustrous, and finely textured foliage. A slow-growing shrub that responds well to pruning, it eventually reaches 5 to 10 feet in height with a usually greater spread, although old specimens can reach 20 feet or more. A wide range of cultivars is available for size, form, and hardiness. 'Black Beauty', 'Hetzii', and 'Helleri' are three of the hardiest, compact types. 'Microphylla' and 'Convexa' are larger, hardier forms. 'Midas Touch' has a variegated yellow margin. 'Beehive' has a compact habit, and 'Dwarf Pagoda' has a very dwarf, compact habit. The Japanese holly makes an excellent selection for hedges, foundation planting, and massing, and for an evergreen, soft texture in the shrub border. It transplants easily into moist, well-drained, slightly acid soils, does well in sun or shade, and appears to be tolerant of pollution. Often sheared into formal shapes; prune after the new growth has matured in the spring. Unlike some hollies, the fruits on this one are black and inconspicuous. Native to Japan.

Ilex glabra

Inkberry
Zones 3 to 10
Broad-leafed evergreen

The inkberry is the hardiest broad-leafed evergreen available to northern gardeners. The dark green foliage grows densely on younger plants in all seasons; older ones can reach 6 to 8 feet in height by 8 to 10 feet in spread and develop a leggy openness. The fruits are black. Plant in moist, acid soil. Prune heavily to renew leggy old plants. This shrub—especially the cultivars 'Compacta', a dwarf, dense type, and 'Nordic', a compact, cold-hardy plant—is excellent for massing, hedges, and foundation planting. Native to swamps from Nova Scotia to Florida and west to Mississippi.

Ilex verticillata

Common winterberry
Zones 4 to 8
Deciduous

This deciduous holly is unusual for its adaptability to wet, swampy soils, to which it

Ilex verticillata (common winterberry)

Ilex vomitoria (yaupon)

is native. A popular plant in the eastern United States, it is an outstanding fruiting shrub, bearing great quantities of bright red berries on bare branches far into the winter. Because birds find the berries tasty, the effective season is limited. Winterberry can grow 20 feet high in the wild, but usually only reaches 6 to 9 feet in the garden, with a similar spread. Plant a male within a few hundred feet of each female to ensure fruiting. Winterberry tolerates dry soil but prefers moist, acid soil high in organic matter. Plant it in full sun to partial shade. Winterberry is particularly effective when planted in large masses, such as in the shrub border and by water. 'Winter Red' is a new cultivar that is superior for its neat, dense growth, 8 to 10 feet high and wide, and for its abundant, bright red fruits. 'Aurantiaca' has orange fruit. 'Red Sprite' is a dwarf with large red fruit. Native from Newfoundland and Minnesota to Georgia, Tennessee, and Missouri.

Ilex vomitoria

Yaupon
Zones 7B to 10
Broad-leafed evergreen

Although the species is a small evergreen tree, several cultivars are available, such as 'Nana' (which has fruit on old wood) and 'Stokes', that are effectively dwarf (18 inches or less) and compact. This holly is more tolerant of alkaline soils and drought than other hollies. Its finely textured foliage can easily be sheared into formal shapes, and although the species is one of the heaviest fruiting of the hollies, the dwarf forms are generally sterile. Native to the southeastern United States.

Juniperus species

Juniper
Hardiness varies according to the species
Conifer

Extremely versatile, available in a vast array of forms and sizes, adaptable to nearly any growing condition, and one of the original low-maintenance plants, *Juniperus* is an immensely popular plant genus. Although they generally require little maintenance, junipers are susceptible to a range of pests, including twig blight, bagworms, white juniper scale, spidermites, spruce mites, twig borers, root rot, and water molds. When planted in shade they quickly become spindly and loose. In wet soils they are especially susceptible to disease. Their large mature size is often disregarded, necessitating removal and replacement that is usually difficult.

Although they are useful as a finely textured evergreen, particularly in the northern garden where such plants are usually in short supply, many varieties of junipers turn dull purple, gray, or dirty green in cold weather.

When properly located and well established, junipers serve a wide range of landscape needs. They prefer sandy, well-drained soil and a sunny, open exposure but grow well in almost any location where the soil is not waterlogged or the shade too deep. Place them away from lawn-oriented sprinklers and avoid overwatering. Most of the species listed below are large trees with a confusing variety of shrublike, prostrate, or columnar cultivars. Some of the most often recommended cultivars follow each species description. Ask local nursery staff which is best for your area, including resistance to pests, and ask about the size to which it will grow.

Juniperus chinensis (Chinese juniper, zones 4 to 10, although cultivars may vary in hardiness)   This is an extremely diverse species, whose cultivars range from prostrate ground covers to 75-foot-high trees. Included under this species are many of the most popular shrublike forms. Most are quite susceptible to Phomopsis blight (especially the cultivar 'San Jose'), which can be devastating in wet years. Beware of the eventual size of many selections—the common 'Pfitzeriana' and 'Hetzii' will grow 15 feet high and 30 feet wide or more. This species prefers alkaline soils. Native to China, Mongolia, and Japan.

Juniperus chinensis 'Pfitzerana Mordigan Aurea' (Chinese juniper)

Juniperus sabina 'Broadmoor' (savin juniper)

Juniperus chinensis 'Procumbens' (Japanese garden juniper, zones 6 to 10)   This is another low, spreading juniper frequently used as a ground cover that spreads over banks and hillsides. Plants grow 1 to 2 feet high and 10 to 15 feet wide at a slow to medium rate. Like *J. horizontalis*, a planting of this juniper can be wiped out by Phomopsis blight. Native to the mountains of Japan.

'Nana' is a dwarf, compact form. 'Armstrong' is a dwarf form that reaches 4 feet high and wide and has soft, gray-green leaves. 'Iowa' is a spreading, relatively open shrub that is 6 feet high and wide at maturity, has bluish green leaves, and is blight resistant. 'Mint Julep' is a dwarf that reaches 2 to 3½ feet high and 6 feet wide and has bright green foliage and blue fruit. The variety *sargentii* grows to 1½ to 2 feet high, spreads 9 to 10 feet wide, has blue-green foliage, and is resistant to Phomopsis blight. 'Sea Spray', a new cultivar that is hardy to zone 5, is often recommended as a substitute for the disease-plagued *J. horizontalis* cultivars because it resists Phomopsis blight, water molds, and root rot. It grows 1 to 2 feet high with a wide spread, and has intense blue-gray foliage.

Juniperus communis (common juniper, zones 2 to 10)   A typical plant of this species is 5 to 10 feet high, spreading 8 to 12 feet, with spiny leaves that are gray or blue-green in the summer, turning to a yellowish or brownish green in winter. All forms of this plant are highly susceptible to Phomopsis blight. Extreme hardiness and adaptability to the poorest, driest soils make it a worthwhile choice for difficult sites.

This species is native to more places than any other tree or shrub in the world, including northern and central Europe, the Mediterranean region, Asia Minor, Iran, Afghanistan, the western Himalayas, Canada, and the eastern United States from New England to Pennsylvania and North Carolina, and west to the Rockies and California.

'Compressa' is a dwarf form growing to 2 to 3 feet, with silvery-green leaves. 'Depressa' requires space to spread as it rarely grows over 4 feet high but often ranges as much as 15 feet wide. 'Depressa Aurea', similar to 'Depressa', has yellow foliage. 'Gold Beach'—suited to rock gardens because it grows to only 6 inches tall and 2 feet wide—has yellow new growth in the spring that changes to green.

Juniperus conferta (shore juniper, zones 6 to 10)   Marked by intense, bluish green, softly textured foliage, this shrub makes an excellent ground cover for coastal gardens. Growing 1 to 2 feet high, it slowly spreads 6 to 8 feet, forming a dense mat. It is tolerant of poor, sandy soils and saline coastal conditions but does not grow well in wet, heavy soil. 'Blue Pacific' and 'Emerald Sea' are two excellent cultivars, due to their extra-low habit and clean, blue-green foliage.

Juniperus horizontalis (creeping juniper, zones 3 to 10)   Almost all of the many cultivars of this low, spreading ground cover turn an unattractive grayish purple in winter. All forms are very susceptible to Phomopsis blight, which, under conditions of high humidity, can devastate entire plantings. Nevertheless, this is a popular species because of several of its blue, prostrate cultivars. Native from Nova Scotia to British Columbia, south to Massachusetts and Montana.

'Bar Harbor', 'Wiltonii' (also known as 'Blue Rug'), and 'Blue Chip' are favorites, with grayish purple winter effects. 'Emerson', a slow-growing form that grows 1 foot high and 9 to 15 feet wide, has blue-green foliage that holds its color throughout the winter.

Juniperus sabina (savin juniper, zones 5 to 10)   The stiff, distinctly vase-shaped branches of this shrub can spread 10 to 15 feet at maturity, with a height of 4 to 6 feet. It is particularly tolerant of urban pollution, and a few of its cultivars are resistant to Phomopsis blight. The lower-growing forms of this plant

Kalmia latifolia (mountain-laurel)

Kerria japonica (Japanese rose)

are excellent for massing, foundation planting, and ground covers. The foliage is a dark green in summer, often turning a brownish green in cold weather. Native to the mountains of central and southern Europe.

'Arcadia', an excellent dwarf form, grows to 1 foot high by 4 feet wide and resists Phomopsis blight. 'Broadmoor' grows 18 inches tall and 10 to 15 feet across in time, building up more height in the center with age, and is also blight resistant. The variety *tamariscifolia* is very popular, although it is susceptible to several pests. 'Skandia' is another blight-resistant shrub, similar to 'Arcadia', with bluish green foliage. 'Von Ehron' is a vase-shaped form growing 5 feet high by 5 feet wide, and is resistant to Phomopsis blight.

Juniperus scopulorum (Rocky Mountain juniper, zones 4 to 10)   Normally a narrow, erect tree that grows 30 to 40 feet high in nature, the smaller cultivars of this plant are valued as hedges, screens, and windbreaks

because of their generally upright habit, slow rate of growth, and bluish cast to the foliage. Native to dry ridges of the higher elevations of the Rocky Mountains, from Alberta to Texas.

'Lakewood Globe' becomes a round 4 to 6 feet after 10 years of growth; it has blue-green foliage. 'Table Top Blue' is a silvery-blue form that grows 5 to 6 feet high and 8 feet wide in 10 years, having a flat-topped appearance. 'Silver Star' is a wide-spreading form, 3 feet high and 6 to 8 feet wide, with silvery-gray foliage. 'Welch' is a narrow, compact column that grows up to 8 feet high and has gray-green new growth that turns blue-green in the summer.

Juniperus virginiana (eastern redcedar, zones 2 to 10) This species is most valued for its many cultivars, all of which are resistant to Phomopsis blight, but which are more susceptible to cedar apple rust and bagworm than most junipers. The foliage ranges from deep green to gray-green, and often assumes a brownish, dull cast in the

winter. Native throughout eastern and central North America.

'Kosteri', a wide-spreading, low-growing form, reaches 3 to 4 feet high and 25 to 30 feet wide after many years and has foliage that turns purplish in the winter and is grayish blue in all other seasons. 'Nana' is a hardy, narrow, upright form that grows 10 to 12 feet high. 'Tripartita' is very similar to a small Pfitzer juniper (see *J. chinensis*). It grows 4 feet tall and 7 feet wide, and has pale green or slightly gray leaves.

Kalmia latifolia

Mountain-laurel
Zones 5 to 8
Broad-leafed evergreen

This is an eastern native with spectacular white to deep pink flowers and excellent evergreen foliage. Use it as a specimen and as a companion for azaleas and rhododendrons. In youth it is dense, rounded, and neat, slowly becoming gnarled, picturesque, and open in old age. In the wild it can reach 30 to 35 feet high, but under

cultivation 7 to 15 feet is a more reasonable figure. In the harsher climate of the Midwest, it rarely grows over a rounded 3 to 7 feet high. Plant it from a container into acid, cool, moist, well-drained soil that is high in organic matter, and give it full sun for optimum flowering. In hot-summer areas, however, partial shade is desirable. Mulch rather than cultivate around its shallow roots. Mountain-laurel is not a good choice for dry, Mediterranean-like climates or areas without frost (zones 9 to 10). Cultivars are available for flower color from white to deep, bright pink. Native from New Brunswick to Indiana and south to Florida and Louisiana.

Kerria japonica

Japanese rose
Zones 5 to 9
Deciduous

For its bright yellow flowers in the spring and bright green stems all winter long, this deciduous shrub performs well in the densest shade. Use it where shade is a problem, in

Kolkwitzia amabilis (beautybush)

Lagerstroemia indica (crapemyrtle)

borders, and in masses and groups. Standing alone, it tends to appear rather disorganized. It grows slowly 3 to 6 feet high and eventually spreads 6 to 9 feet. Keep this tough, carefree shrub away from rich, fertile soils where it decreases flower production. Plant it in deep to partial shade, because its flowers fade quickly in full sun. A protected location with good drainage reduces the chance of winter damage. Prune directly after flowering as it flowers on last year's wood. 'Pleniflora' is the most popular cultivar, being double flowered and extremely showy. Native to western and central China.

Kolkwitzia amabilis

Beautybush
Zones 5 to 8
Deciduous

A low-maintenance, traditional shrub of limited value when not in flower, the beautybush is nevertheless quite a spectacle in bloom. Bright pink flowers are produced in profusion in late May. It is a large shrub with medium texture in the summer and coarse texture in the winter. It grows rapidly to 6 to 10 feet high (sometimes 12 feet) and has a slightly smaller spread. The upright arching form usually becomes leggy, but the reddish, peeling bark of the lower trunks and branches can be attractive. Nevertheless, this shrub is best used in the rear of the shrub border in large gardens. Easily transplanted, it is indifferent to soil type or pH. Give it a sunny location and plenty of room to grow, and prune out older stems every year. Old, overgrown shrubs can be renewed by cutting them completely to the ground. Prune after flowering as it blooms on old wood. Native to central China.

Lagerstroemia indica

Crapemyrtle
Zones 7B to 10
Deciduous

Brilliant floral displays in late summer and early fall, spectacular fall foliage color, and attractive, mottled bark in the winter make this an all-season plant. Actually a small tree, most forms can be grown as a large upright-rounded shrub, 15 to 25 feet high and as wide, and several dwarf cultivars 5 to 12 feet tall are available. It makes a handsome specimen or focal grouping, particularly with a ground cover planted underneath it. This shrub can also be effective integrated into a foundation planting or as a hedge or screen. New foliage is bronze, maturing to a medium green, then turning into electric reds, yellows, or oranges in the fall. Flowers are produced from July to September in great profusion. A wide variety of cultivars are available that have white, pink, deep red, and lavender blooms. Crapemyrtle flowers on the current season's growth, so it can be pruned as late as early spring and still produce flowers the same season. Plant it in well-drained, moist soil rich in organic matter and in a hot, sunny location. Spray to control aphids. Try to select from the newer dwarf cultivars developed by the National Arboretum for resistance to powdery mildew. Otherwise, you will need to spray just prior to blooming every year to control this disease. Prune annually to increase flowering wood by removing flower clusters and small twiggy growth on small shrubs, or 12 to 18 inches of each branch on large ones. Older, overgrown plants can be cut clear to the ground to renew or contain them. Native to China and Korea.

Leptospermum scoparium

New Zealand tea-tree
Zones 9 to 10
Narrow-leafed evergreen

For an outstanding floral display from late winter to spring and an accent of finely textured, fragrant evergreen foliage, the New Zealand tea-tree can be effective in gardens with a mild climate, particularly the Mediterranean-like climates of the West Coast. Variable from seed, it is available in a range of cultivars for flower color (in reds, pinks, and white) and habit (from 6 to 10 feet high to

Leptospermum scoparium 'Nanum Kea' (New Zealand tea-tree)

Leucothoe fontanesiana (drooping leucothoe)

Ligustrum lucidum (glossy privet)

prostrate ground covers 8 to 12 inches high and 2 to 3 feet wide). The flowers are profuse and colorful, appearing from late winter to midsummer, depending on the variety, and are effective for about two to four weeks.

Leptospermum scoparium must have thorough drainage and prefers a location in full sun. Once established, it is drought tolerant and pest-free. Shear or prune lightly for a formal appearance. Never prune into bare wood, as this prevents buds from breaking into new growth. An excellent choice in seacoast gardens as a specimen, accent, or focal point in the shrub border. The prostrate forms make interesting and colorful ground covers, although they do not suppress weeds. Native to New Zealand.

Leucothoe fontanesiana

Drooping leucothoe
Zones 5 to 7
Broad-leafed evergreen

Most commonly planted in moist, acid eastern gardens, the drooping leucothoe makes

a fine companion to rhododendrons, azaleas, and mountain-laurel because of its evergreen, lustrous, dark foliage and graceful form. The bright green or bronze new foliage in the spring and the purplish winter color, along with the delicate, subtle, white, fragrant flowers in spring, are assets. Use leucothoe as a background plant for leggy shrubs, a graceful high ground cover for shady slopes, or for massing, or integrating into the shrub border. It is a perfect shrub to naturalize in a shady woodland wildflower garden.

Leucothoe fontanesiana transplants easily from a container in early spring. If given an acid, moist, well-drained soil that is high in organic matter, as well as full shade, ample moisture, and protection from drought and drying winds, it is a nearly trouble-free plant. Prune directly after flowering, although pruning is seldom necessary due to its graceful, fountainlike form, which grows 3 to 5 feet high

and often wider. Rejuvenate older plants by pruning to the ground.

'Girard's Rainbow' has yellow, green, and copper-variegated foliage, 'Nana' is a dwarf form. Native to streamsides in the mountains of Virginia to North Carolina and Tennessee.

Ligustrum species

Privet
Hardiness varies with species
Some evergreen, some deciduous species

Pest-free, highly adaptable, and low in maintenance, the shrubby privets are most often used as formal and informal hedges, backgrounds, and screens. Most have white, spikelike clusters of strongly scented flowers in early summer. The scent is variously described as offensive to pleasant, so smell before you buy. All privets transplant easily from bare roots, are adaptable to nearly any soil except a wet one, and take full sun to partial shade. They perform well under adverse conditions of pollution and

drought. If flowers are desired, prune just after blooming; otherwise, prune any time. All privets are rapidly growing shrubs that respond well to pruning and shaping.

Ligustrum amurense (Amur privet, zones 4 to 10, deciduous) A hardy privet that is excellent for hedges, it has good, clean, medium- to fine-textured foliage. Native to northern China.

Ligustrum japonicum (Japanese privet, zones 7B to 10, evergreen) Japanese privet makes an excellent hedge or screen in southern or western gardens because of its evergreen, lustrous leaves, its dense, compact habit (it grows rapidly 6 to 12 feet high), and its responsiveness to pruning. It is also commonly used for training into topiary or small standards. An excellent container plant, it looks best when given plenty of water and protected from the hot sun. Many forms are available. This plant is frequently sold incorrectly in nurseries as *Ligustrum texanum*. Native to Japan and Korea.

Lonicera tatarica (Tartarian honeysuckle)

Magnolia stellata (star magnolia)

Ligustrum lucidum (glossy privet, zones 7B to 10, evergreen)   Often confused with the Japanese privet, this privet is more treelike growing 35 to 40 feet high. To differentiate it from *L. japonicum* among young nursery plants, feel the undersides of the leaves. If the veins are raised, it is *L. japonicum;* if they are sunken, it is *L. lucidum.* Native to China and Korea.

Ligustrum obtusifolium (border privet, zones 4 to 10, deciduous)   In addition to being one of the hardiest privets, the border privet is also one of the most attractive because of its broad, horizontal growth habit and dark green foliage. It grows 10 to 12 feet tall and 12 to 15 feet wide, although it can easily be kept much smaller. The variety *regelianum* is a low, 4- to 5-foot-high shrub with unusual, horizontally spreading branches that are most attractive if allowed to grow naturally. Native to Japan.

Ligustrum ovalifolium (California privet, zones 6 to 10, deciduous)   This privet

has excellent glossy, semi-evergreen leaves. Although it dies to the ground every winter in northern zones, where hardy it is a popular hedge plant. Native to Japan.

Ligustrum 'Suwanee River' (zones 7B to 10, evergreen) This fine evergreen hybrid eventually grows 4 to 6 feet high, with a compact, tight habit. Its dark green, wavy leaves are useful as a low hedge or in a foundation planting.

Ligustrum 'Vicaryi' (golden privet, zones 6 to 10, deciduous)   In full sun the leaves are a glaring yellow; in shade they are yellow-green to light green. Clipped hedges remain yellow-green, because the shaded inner leaves are constantly exposed from clipping. 'Hillside Strain' is a hardier variety that is useful in zone 5, although it is a difficult, gaudy plant to integrate into the landscape.

Ligustrum vulgare (common privet, zones 5 to 10, deciduous)   This is a plant to avoid because of its susceptibility to anthracnose.

Lonicera tatarica

Tartarian honeysuckle
Zones 3B to 9
Deciduous

The chief attributes of this shrub are intensely fragrant, early May flowers that are available in the widest color range (whites, pinks, and reds), of any honeysuckle and showy, bright red berries in June. The bluish green, dense foliage has a medium texture. This shrub becomes quite leggy and, like nearly all honeysuckles, is unattractive in winter; use in the shrub border where these factors can be hidden. An upright and arching shrub that is 10 to 12 feet high and wide, the berries are a favorite of birds, who deposit them all over the garden so that it is soon full of seedlings. Easily transplanted and adaptable to many soils, *L. tatarica* prefers full sun. Prune just after flowering. Renew overgrown plants by cutting to the ground. 'Arnold Red' has the darkest red flowers of any honeysuckle. 'Nana'

has pink flowers and grows only 3 feet high. Native to central Asia.

Lonicera nitida (box honeysuckle, zones 7B to 10)   This fine-textured evergreen bears fragrant white flowers in June. Tolerant of coastal conditions, this shrub responds well to pruning and makes an excellent hedge. Unlike other honeysuckles, it presents a neat, refined appearance.

Lonicera × *xylosteoides* 'Clavey's Dwarf' (zones 5 to 10)   Excellent for a low hedge, it forms a neat, 3- to 6-foot mound. 'Emerald Mound' is a low-growing type with bluish green leaves, becoming 3 feet high and 4 to 6 feet wide.

Magnolia quinquepeta (formerly M. liliiflora)

Lily magnolia
Zones 6 to 10
Deciduous

The large, showy flowers of the lily magnolia are purple on the outside with white centers, and effective from late April to early May (earlier in mild

Mahonia aquifolium (Oregon grapeholly)

Mahonia bealei (leatherleaf mahonia)

climates). A smaller, more open shrub than the star magnolia (*M. stellata*), it grows slowly to 8 to 12 feet in height with a similar spread. Treat it the same as the star magnolia for culture and landscape use. Several cultivars are available, the most popular being 'Nigra,' which has larger, deeper purple flowers and a more restrained habit. Native to China.

Magnolia stellata

Star magnolia
Zones 5 to 10
Deciduous

Especially when displayed against a dark background the large, white, fragrant flowers of the star magnolia are glorious in early to mid-April (March in the south). It grows slowly to 15 to 20 feet tall and 10 to 15 feet wide, and it is often planted without consideration for its large ultimate size. Use it as a specimen, in groups, or focused in the shrub border or foundation planting. The flowers are delicate and often damaged by wind and rain, but late frosts present

the most danger because of the early blooming period. Put them in a protected location, and avoid southern exposures, which force the flowers out even earlier. Plant magnolias in the spring in deep, rich, well-drained and moist soil, and never cultivate around the roots—they are fleshy and close to the surface and are easily damaged. Do not plant the crown below the soil level. Give magnolias full sun to partial shade. Pruning, although rarely necessary, should be done immediately after flowering. Native to Japan.

'Rosea' has pink buds that open into white flowers; 'Pink Star' has flowers that remain clear pink. *Magnolia* × 'Ann' is a new hybrid that has fragrant, lilylike, pink buds and pink flowers that open later and last longer than the star magnolia. It also displays a superior, uniform 8- to-12-foot upright habit. Although better form and flower are important considerations, its chief advantage is a later flowering period, and hence decreased susceptibility to late frosts.

Mahonia aquifolium

Oregon grapeholly
Zones 5 to 9
Broad-leafed evergreen

Mahonia aquifolium is an open, loose shrub with upright, heavy stems and very showy, bright yellow flowers in late April. Popular as an evergreen ground cover in shady areas, its irregular spreading habit and high growth (3 to 6 feet wide and sometimes 9 feet tall) are best when integrated into a shrub border or foundation planting, and possibly as a specimen. Although its spiny, hollylike leaves are evergreen, the leaves often turn a purplish bronze in cold weather. In locations that are exposed to wind and sun, they scorch and turn brown. It is inclined to spread by underground stems. The shrub's tendency to openness and straggliness can be controlled by pruning annually just after flowering to maintain a 3-foot height. Plant in a moist, acid soil and protect it from hot sun and wind. Several cultivars are available for better form, winter leaf colors, and floriferousness.

Native to damp forests from British Columbia to Oregon.

Mahonia bealei

Leatherleaf mahonia
Zones 6B to 10
Broad-leafed evergreen

Striking structural interest is the chief attribute of this plant. It often grows 10 to 12 feet high and has strongly vertical, little-branched stems and large, compound leaves that are held horizontally. The effect is exotic and tropical, especially when displayed against a wall or dramatically lit at night. In addition, it produces large, showy clusters of yellow flowers, followed by powdery blue, grapelike fruit. This mahonia does not tolerate drought, hot sun, or winter sun and wind, and should be planted in a rich, moist soil and given plenty of water. Consider its ultimate size before planting as it is difficult to prune correctly. Native to China.

Mahonia lomariifolia (zones 8B to 10)   Although more tender than *M. bealei,* this

Malus sargentii (Sargent's crabapple)

Myrica pensylvanica (northern bayberry)

Myrtus communis 'Variegata' (myrtle)

shrub is even more dramatic, with larger, coarser foliage. Both of these mahonias make excellent container plants. Avoid planting where the spiny foliage can scratch people. Native to China.

Malus sargentii

Sargent's crabapple
Zones 5 to 9
Deciduous

Most crabapples are thought of as trees; this one is small enough to be used as a shrub. This easy-to-grow plant is strongly horizontal, growing 6 to 8 feet tall and spreading twice as wide. It has white, fragrant flowers in mid-May, which are the most effective in alternate years; dark green foliage in the summer; and bright red, pea-sized crabapples in the fall and early winter that are adored by birds. It is adaptable to a wide variety of soils, preferring full sun and average watering. Although it is seldom necessary, prune directly after flowering and before next year's buds set in mid-June.

'Tina' is an extremely dwarf form, 18 to 24 inches high and 2 to 3 feet wide. 'Rosea' has clear pink buds. *M. sargentii* is highly resistant to many of the diseases that commonly plague crabapples. Native to Japan.

Myrica pensylvanica

Northern bayberry
Zones 2 to 7
Deciduous

Bayberry is one of the few plants outside of the pea family that fixes its own nitrogen from the atmosphere and that actually prefers infertile, dry, sandy soils. It is excellent for large-scale massing in poor soil and coastal areas and adapts well to difficult urban sites, where it forms masses of deep, lustrous green foliage, ranging from 5 to 12 feet in height. It tends to sucker and form large colonies, but is also good for a shrub border or informal hedge or for combining the broad-leafed evergreens. The fruits are grayish white, waxy berries that are produced in great quantities along the stems of female plants and

persist all winter long. All parts of the plant are aromatic—the berries have been used since colonial times to make fragrant candles. Transplant from a container into any soil and give it full sun to partial shade. It is tolerant of salt spray and wind, and it attracts no serious pests. Older, leggy plants can be renewed by pruning down to the ground. Native to coastal areas from Newfoundland to North Carolina, and along the Great Lakes.

Myrtus communis

Myrtle
Zones 9 to 10
Broad-leafed evergreen

With glossy bright green foliage—fragrant when bruised—myrtles are commonly used in the hot, dry areas and coastal gardens of Arizona and California as formal or informal hedges, screens, masses, or backgrounds. Myrtle shears well and is easily trained into a formal hedge. Unpruned, the myrtle is usually seen as a 5- to 6-foot-high and 4- to 5-foot-

wide, round, bushy shrub, although it can attain treelike dimensions with great age, up to 15 feet tall and 20 feet wide. Sweet-scented flowers are produced in the summer. The smooth, rusty-tan bark is showy on older specimens. Other than requiring fast drainage, it is not particular about soil. Many cultivars are available, mostly for form and foliage color. Native to the Mediterranean region.

Nandina domestica

Nandina, heavenly-bamboo
Zones 7 to 10
Broad-leafed evergreen
(semideciduous in the north)

Despite its name, nandina is not even remotely related to bamboo. It is a deservedly popular shrub in southern gardens for its variety of ornamental assets and easy care. A strongly vertical form contrasts nicely with delicate, wispy foliage that is evergreen in mild climates. Erect, creamy white flower spikes borne on the ends of the vertical branches in June are followed by bright red clusters of

Nandina domestica (nandina, heavenly-bamboo)

Nerium oleander (oleander)

Osmanthus fragrans (sweet olive)

berries. Even with only a few hours of sun a day, nandina frequently has brilliant crimson to purple foliage in the fall and winter. Often reaching 8 feet in height and 2½ to 3 feet in width, nandina is effective as a hedge or screen, in a mass or grouping, and as a specimen in an entryway or container. It is particularly effective when backlit. Nandina loses its leaves at 10° F, and dies back to the ground at 0° F, although it quickly recovers the following season. In the northern limits of its range, it is best used as an herbaceous perennial. Because cross-fertilization improves fruiting, plant nandina in groups. It performs well in nearly any soil, in sun or shade (although protection is required in hot climates), and established plants tolerate drought well. Prune out old, leggy canes annually to encourage density. Nandina is little troubled by pests, but exhibits chlorosis in alkaline soils. Several cultivars are offered for form, dwarf size, foliage color, and hardiness. 'Harbor Dwarf' and 'Gulf Stream' are both excellent

cultivars. Native to central China and Japan.

Nerium oleander

Oleander
Zones 8 to 10
Broad-leafed evergreen

This is a commonly used shrub in the South and west of the Rockies because of its coarse evergreen foliage, attractive red, pink, white, or yellow flowers in the summer, and easy care, especially in hot, dry climates. A broad, rounded, and bulky shrub, oleander grows very rapidly to 8 to 12 feet tall and 6 to 10 feet wide, sometimes becoming open and leggy. Plant oleander in full sun, in any soil from dry sand to wet clay. Tolerant of heat, salt, and drought, it is an excellent choice for desert gardens. Prune the shrub in early spring to control size and form. Remove old wood that has flowered each year. Tip-pinch to encourage density, or pull off suckers from the base to encourage more open height. Oleander is plagued by many insects and diseases, particularly in shady or humid

environments. Mildew, scale, and aphids are among the most severe.

All parts of the plant are violently poisonous. Be extremely cautious with clippings from pruning. Smoke from burning plant parts, green or dried, can cause severe skin and respiratory irritations. Contact with leaves can cause dermatitis. Ingesting even small amounts can cause severe illness, even death. Many cultivars are available for flower color, fragrance, and dwarf habit. Native to the Mediterranean region.

Osmanthus fragrans

Sweet olive
Zones 8 to 10
Broad-leafed evergreen

Although its powerfully fragrant, nearly year-round flowers are a primary attraction, sweet olive is also useful as a compact, neat plant with glossy evergreen foliage that makes an outstanding hedge, screen, background, espalier, or container plant. It is very

easy to care for and quite adaptable. Plant *Osmanthus fragrans* in any soil, from sand to clay, give it partial shade, and it grows at a moderate rate to a shrub 10 feet wide and high with a rounded outline. It can easily be kept lower, however, and responds well to shearing. Prune any time of the year; pinch the growing tips to encourage denseness. 'Aurianticus' has orange blossoms that concentrate their bloom in October and will astound you with their powerful fragrance. Native to eastern Asia.

Osmanthus delavayi
(Delavay osmanthus, zones 8 to 10)   Small, finely textured leaves and a graceful, arching habit distinguish this *Osmanthus*, along with the largest white flowers of the genus. They are profuse and fragrant from late March to May. Particularly handsome on banks and walls where branches can cascade, it also responds well to pruning as a hedge or foundation plant.

Osmanthus heterophyllus
(holly olive, zones 7 to 10) This is perhaps the most hand-

Paeonia suffruticosa (tree peony)

some of the *Osmanthus* species and is often confused with English holly. Holly has alternate leaves whereas *Osmanthus* always has opposite leaves. Possessing lustrous, spiny, dark green leaves and fragrant, hidden, yellow flowers in the fall, it is available in a number of cultivars for variegated foliage. This *Osmanthus* is unusually shade tolerant. 'Variegatus' is an excellent cultivar.

Paeonia suffruticosa

Tree peony
Zones 5 to 9
Deciduous

Although the curiously textured foliage on this deciduous, woody shrub is an asset, the tree peony is grown chiefly for its enormous flower, 6 to 10 inches or more in diameter, with exquisitely intergraded coloring and a delicate texture like crepe paper. A colorful array of cultivars and hybrids are available. Usually growing to a rather open, leggy shrub, 4 feet high and wide and sometimes larger, the leaves are in proportion to the flow-

ers—equally huge, often 18 inches long. The deeply cut lobes, however, impart a curious mixture of coarse and fine texture to the plant. The blossoms last 10 days at most. Single or semidouble forms are preferable; the fully double blossoms are so heavy they require individual staking.

Plant tree peonies in early fall in well-drained, moist, rich soil that has been amended with ample organic matter to make it slightly alkaline (although they tolerate slight acidity). These plants live a long time, so carefully preparing the soil in the beginning pays off in the long run. Choose their positions in the garden carefully as they do not transplant well. Grafted forms must be planted with the graft union at least 4 inches below the ground, so that the grafts may form their own roots. Protect from rabbits during the first year by covering them with wire cages, and mulch well. Carpenter bees are a serious pest in the East; control them by plugging entry holes or cutting the plant back to the ground and

destroying the refuse. Don't mulch after the first year, and remove fading blossoms immediately to help control botrytis fungus. Native from Bhutan to Tibet and China.

Paxistima canbyi

Canby paxistima, cliffgreen
Zones 5B to 8
Broad-leafed evergreen

Canby paxistima is most popular in the gardens of the Northeast and Pacific Northwest as an excellent evergreen ground cover. It grows 12 to 24 inches high and spreads slowly to 3 to 5 feet. Its lustrous, dark green leaves change to an attractive bronze in the winter. Paxistima is a finely textured, neat, and compact shrub that is useful as a facing for taller shrubs, as an edging plant, or as a low hedge. The flowers and fruit are inconspicuous. Best bought in a container, it is easily transplanted into moist, well-drained, acid soil. It is found on rocky soil in the wild, but under cultivation it seems to do best in soils that are high in organic matter. Denser and

more compact in full sun, it tolerates partial shade well. Leave alone once established as it rarely requires feeding or pruning and has no severe pests. Grow in regions of high atmospheric moisture. Native to rocky woods and slopes in the mountains of West Virginia, Ohio, and Kentucky.

Philadelphus coronarius

Sweet mockorange
Zones 5 to 8
Deciduous

Although its white, late-May flowers are known for their powerful fragrance and have long been popular, the sweet mockorange has little else to offer. Usually a coarse, leggy, and straggly shrub that grows rapidly to an upright and irregular 10 to 12 feet in height and width, even the smaller cultivars are unattractive when they are not in flower (about 50 weeks out of the year). It is easy to grow, free from serious pests, not particular about soil, and performs well in sun or partial shade. Its wide-ranging root system is

Philadelphus coronarius (sweet mockorange)

Picea abies 'Nidiformis' (bird's-nest spruce)

highly competitive. Prune annually immediately after it completes flowering by removing all older wood, or even cutting it to the ground. Use *Philadelphus* where its fragrance can be appreciated—in the border, near outdoor living areas, entryways, and windows. Many of the mockoranges offered by nurseries are not as fragrant as others, so select for fragrance only when the plants are in flower. Native to Europe and southwestern Asia.

Philadelphus × 'Frosty Morn' (zone 4)   This new hybrid has double flowers that rival *P.* × *lemoinei* for fragrance.

Philadelphus × *lemoinei* (zones 6 to 8)   Among the cultivars of this hybrid are some of the best choices for fragrance, including 'Avalanche' (4 feet tall with single white flowers), 'Girandole' (4 feet tall with double flowers), and 'Innocence' (8 feet tall with single flowers).

Philadelphus × *virginalis* This hybrid also has many cultivars, which are generally less fragrant than *P. coronarius* or *P.* × *lemoinei*, but many of which are hardier (to zone 4 or 5). 'Minnesota Snowflake' is a fragrant one, 6 feet high and hardy to zone 4.

Photinia × fraseri

No common name
Zones 7B to 10
Broad-leafed evergreen

This evergreen shrub is best known for its bright, bronzy-red, new foliage in the spring. It also produces ivory flowers in 4-inch clusters in late March and April. If unpruned, it grows to a rounded shrub 10 feet tall and somewhat wider, but it is easily restrained. Use it as a screen, formal or informal hedge, or espalier, or train it into a single-stemmed small tree. Its lustrous, dark green foliage makes an excellent background. Although not fruiting as profusely as other photinias, its red berries are attractive to birds. Plant photinias in well-drained soil that has been amply amended with organic matter. Even though they are heat resistant in the desert, they should be watered generously. Do not splash water on the leaves, which are susceptible to fireblight. If fireblight occurs, the ends of branches appear blackened, as if burned. Carefully prune them out, sterilizing the shears in alcohol or bleach after each cut, and destroy the refuse. Spray regularly for aphids and scale.

Photinia serrulasta (Chinese photinia, zones 7B to 10) This is a large shrub or small tree that grows 36 feet high. Its large, coarsely textured leaves make a good screen. The dull white flowers are profuse in the spring; they gradually change to brownish pink and are quite showy. These are followed by red berries.

Picea abies 'Nidiformis'

Bird's-nest spruce
Zones 2 to 4 (limited use south of zone 6B)
Conifer

This is a popular dwarf spruce that makes a dense, low, flat-topped evergreen cushion, 3 to 6 feet high and 4 to 8 feet wide. It is useful as a specimen in rock gardens, entryways, or other focal spots. Preferring well-drained, sandy, and moderately moist soil, it tolerates others as long as there is sufficient moisture. The further south below zone 5 it is planted, the weaker it becomes, as it prefers the moist climates of deep winter cold and summer coolness. It does not perform well in hot, dry, windy locations. Like all spruces, it is best in full sun or light shade. This spruce is also a poor choice for polluted urban environments. Many other choice dwarf forms of the spruce are available, from low and wide spreading to erect or pendulous, but this is the most common one. Native to northern and central Europe.

Picea albertiana glauca 'Conica'   (Dwarf Alberta spruce, zones 2 to 7, conifer) A stiffly conical and extremely slow-growing (about 1 to 2 inches per year) dwarf, often described as looking like an upside-down ice cream cone. It may eventually reach 6 to 8 feet in extreme old age. The

Pieris japonica (lily-of-the-valley shrub)

Pinus mugo var. *mugo* (dwarf mountain pine)

Pittosporum tobira (Japanese pittosporum)

finely textured, light-green needles and unusual form make this an interesting specimen best used in a focal grouping. Especially in hot, dry areas, it is very susceptible to red spidermites. A heavy shower with a strong stream of water helps to control this problem. For severe infestations, a miticide is necessary. Native to northern North America.

Pieris japonica

Lily-of-the-valley shrub
Zones 6 to 9
Broad-leafed evergreen

A broad-leafed evergreen related to rhododendrons and kalmias, the lily-of-the-valley shrub is grown for its delicate, whitish or pinkish white, pendulous panicles of flowers that bloom in early spring (mid-to late March) and that last for two to three weeks, and for its deep green foliage with bronze-red new growth in the spring. It grows slowly to a 9- to 12-foot height and 6- to 8-foot spread, with an upright, irregular, and rounded outline. Use pieris as a specimen, in

the shrub border, or in groups or masses. It combines well with other acid-loving, broad-leafed evergreens, and integrates well into a foundation planting. Preferring moist, acid soil, it is not as particular as other members of the heath family. Protect it from wind and winter sun, especially in cold-winter areas. When pruning is necessary, which is seldom, do so just after flowering. Leaf spots, a dieback fungus, lace bugs, scale, and mites can be severe problems. In the northern limits of its range and in exposed situations, the flower buds, which are naked all winter, are often killed. Several cultivars are available for more compact form, pink flowers, and unusual foliage color and texture. Native to Japan.

Pieris floribunda (mountain pieris fetterbush, zones 5 to 8) Hardier, lower, and bushier than *P. japonica* (growing 2 to 6 feet high with a similar spread), this pieris has upright panicles of fragrant white flowers in April. Additional attributes include

greater resistance to lace bugs and tolerance of higher pH levels. Unfortunately, it is rarely available. Native to cool, damp mountain slopes from Virginia to Georgia.

Pieris forrestii (Chinese pieris, zones 8B to 10) This shrub is more tender than *Pieris japonica,* with showy scarlet foliage, larger leaves, and a denser, larger habit. Native to China.

Pinus mugo var. mugo

Dwarf mountain pine
Zones 2 to 8 (but not in the desert)
Conifer

It is often sold for its diminutive cushion shape 2 to 4 feet high, but grows to be a 10-foot-tall, 15-foot-wide plant when mature. If a reliably small plant is desired, consider the hard-to-find cultivars, such as 'Compacta', 'Gnome', or 'Slavinii'. The dwarf mountain pine, however, can be pruned annually by removing approximately two thirds of each young, expanding candle in

the spring to maintain a compact, dense form. Use it for textural evergreen interest in a foundation planting, as low masses, or in groupings. Plant it in moist, deep loam in full sun or partial shade. Many other dwarf pines are becoming available. Such dwarf pines include selected cultivars of *Pinus strobus* (white pine), and *Pinus sylvestris* (Scotch pine). *Pinus mugo* is native to the mountains of Europe, from Spain to the Balkans.

Pittosporum tobira

Japanese pittosporum
Zones 8B to 10
Broad-leafed evergreen

Dark green, clean, leathery evergreen foliage; fragrant, early, creamy yellow spring flowers with a scent like orange blossoms; and a broad, dense habit all have made this a popular plant in southern and western gardens for screens, massing, borders, and foundation planting. It is particularly effective in containers or trained as a small, crooked-stemmed tree. This

Potentilla fruticosa (bush-cinquefoil)

Prunus laurocerasus (English laurel)

Platycladus orientalis (Oriental arborvitae)

pittosporum does not respond well to hard pruning or shearing, although frequent light pinching can help to maintain a compact habit. Allowed to grow naturally, it reaches 6 to 15 feet in height and is usually slightly wider. Fairly drought resistant, it nevertheless appreciates adequate water and an annual light fertilization. Aphids and scale can be a problem. Full sun to partial shade is best, although it tolerates dense shade well. Native to Japan and China.

Pittosporum crassifolium (karo, zones 9 to 10)   This large shrub grows up to 25 feet high, although it can easily be held to a 6-foot hedge. The finely textured, gray-green foliage responds well to shearing and tolerates wind and coastal salts. 'Nana' is a 3-foot dwarf.

Pittosporum eugenoides (tarata, zones 9 to 10)   This popular hedge plant, has wavy-edged, glossy, light green leaves that respond well to shearing. Yellow, fragrant flowers are produced on unpruned plants.

Pittosporum napaulense (golden-fragrance plant, zones 9 to 10)   This coarsely textured shrub grows to 12 feet high and 8 feet wide. Grow this one for its excellent spring display of profuse, golden yellow flowers and powerful fragrance.

Platycladus orientalis (formerly Thuja orientalis)

Oriental arborvitae
Zones 7 to 10
Conifer

Like the American arborvitae, this species is a 50-foot tree from which many dwarf, shrublike cultivars have been developed. Many of the dwarf cultivars are popular in the South, especially the bright yellow- or blue-foliaged forms. 'Aurea Nana' is a rounded yellow dwarf; 'Blue Spire' is a pyramidal form with blue leaves. The Oriental arborvitae, besides being more tender, differs from the American arborvitae in the distinctly vertical, fan-shaped planes of its branches. Although it is tolerant of drier

soils and less atmospheric moisture, it still needs protection from harsh, dry winds. Native to northern China and Korea.

Potentilla fruticosa

Bush-cinquefoil
Zones 2 to 8
Deciduous

The bush-cinquefoil is one of the most versatile shrubs, suitable in a shrub border, as a foundation planting, for massing and edging, and as a low, informal hedge or facing plant. Its bright yellow, 1-inch flowers are abundant from June until frost. Its dense, upright stems grow slowly to a neat, rounded plant, 1 to 4 feet high and 2 to 4 feet wide. Its delicate, finely textured, deciduous foliage is a handsome bright green. Bush-cinquefoil grows well in any soil from wet to dry, heavy to light. It tolerates extreme cold and drought, is virtually free from pests (although occasionally susceptible to mites during dry spells), and requires no pruning. It flowers most abundantly in full sun,

but tolerates partial shade well. It is one of the most carefree plants around. Many cultivars are available in a range of flower colors (white, yellow, orange, or red), sizes, and foliage color (bright green to gray-green). Orange- and redflowering varieties fade in full sun, so plant in partial shade. Native to meadows and bogs, northern and mountainous Asia, Europe, and North America.

Prunus laurocerasus

English laurel
Zones 7 to 10
Broad-leafed evergreen

Grown for its large, dark, evergreen leaves, this large shrub or small tree is most commonly seen as a formal hedge, screen, or background plant in southern gardens. Give it partial shade (except on the coast) and protect it from scale and fungal leaf spots with regular spraying. It is not particular about soil. Left unpruned, in southern climates it has been known to grow 25 or 30 feet tall. In northern climates, 4 to 6 feet is more

Prunus tomentosa (Nanking cherry, Manchu cherry)

Punica granatum 'Wonderful' (pomegranate)

likely. Expect high maintenance as a clipped hedge, due to its extremely rapid growth rate. Shearing mutilates the large leaves, so it is better to prune selectively. Beware of its greedy, far-reaching roots. Native to southeastern Europe and Asia Minor. 'Schipkaensis' is hardy to zone 6, with protection. It has smaller leaves and grows 9 feet tall. 'Otto Luyken' is another excellent, low-growing form, hardy to zone 6B.

Prunus tomentosa

Nanking cherry, Manchu cherry

Zones 2 to 8

Deciduous

One of the most handsome of the deciduous shrubby cherries, this is a broad shrub that reaches an open 6- to 10-foot height and 15-foot spread. It accepts shearing well, making a dense hedge, although the fruits are sacrificed. The bark is a shiny, exfoliating, reddish brown and a distinct attraction in the winter. But the chief beauty of this shrub lies in its pink buds that open into white, fragrant flowers

in early to mid-April (March in mild climates), followed by scarlet fruits that are deliciously edible. Use this plant as a specimen, a hedge in groups and masses, or in a shrub border. 'Holly Jolivette' grows as a large to small tree and has open white double flowers. Native to the Himalayas.

Prunus × cistena (purple-leaf sand cherry, zones 2 to 7) Valuable for its extreme hardiness and intensely reddish-purple foliage that holds its color all summer long, it has pinkish, fragrant May flowers and blackish fruits that are of secondary importance. This is a small shrub that grows rapidly to an upright and irregular 8 to 10 feet.

Prunus glandulosa (dwarf flowering almond, zones 5 to 8) Unattractive when not in flower, this is a straggly, 4- to 5-foot-high, upright shrub commonly grown due to its ease of propagation.

Prunus maritima (beach plum, zones 4 to 7) This generally inferior, rounded, dense, 6-foot-high bush is useful for

its tolerance to the salt sprays and sandy soils of the seacoast. The fruits are delicious and follow white early May flowers. Varieties have been selected for larger fruits.

Prunus triloba (flowering almond, zones 6 to 9) This large, treelike shrub growing 12 to 15 feet high is chiefly attractive when in bloom. The flowers are small, pinkish, double, and roselike in late April (earlier in the South), and are borne in large quantities. Unfortunately, they are frequently killed just as they are opening by a late freeze.

Punica granatum

Pomegranate

Zones 8 to 10

Deciduous

A deciduous shrub valuable for its showy, waxy orange or scarlet flowers in July and August and brilliant yellow autumn foliage, a few varieties will also produce delicious fruits. It is an excellent desert shrub, quite tolerant of heat and alkaline soils, that withstands considerable drought if the quality of the fruit is

unimportant. *P. granatum* arches to a fountainlike height of 12 to 15 feet and forms a dense, twiggy mass. Several cultivars are available for flower variation, from a single or double scarlet to white, yellow, and red. Selections are also available for fruit quality ('Wonderful' is the most popular form for fruit), and for size, ranging from 18-inch container or edging plants to 15-foot border shrubs. Plant in full sun for best blooms and fruit. The fruit is best when the shrub is watered regularly Native from southeastern Europe across Asia to the Himalayas.

Pyracantha coccinea

Scarlet firethorn

Zones 6B to 10

Broad-leafed evergreen (semideciduous in the North)

Showy white flowers in the spring, excellent evergreen or semievergreen foliage, and vivid red or orange fruit in the fall and winter are features of this all-season shrub. The form is irregular, with varieties ranging from upright to

Pyracantha coccinea (scarlet firethorn)

Raphiolepis indica (India-hawthorn)

prostrate. Several dwarf forms are available. It grows to 6 to 18 feet in height and spread, and the sharp thorns make an impenetrable barrier. Useful as a specimen, screen, or barrier hedge, it is an especially popular espalier against walls and along fences. Because of its mature size and thorniness, pyracantha is not suited to planting next to doors, drives, walks, or patios. The thorns also make it very difficult to prune, so give it plenty of room to grow. This is an easy plant to grow in full sun and well-drained soil, but don't move it after it is established. Guard against standing water on its foliage at bloomtime, because fireblight is a serious problem. Scale, aphids, spidermites, apple scab, and lace bug can also be damaging. Native from Italy to western Asia.

Most of the available cultivars are hardy only to zone 7. 'Kasan', 'Lalandei', 'Thornless', 'Wyattii', and 'Chadwickii' are all hardy to zone 6. 'Teton' is a new, strongly vertical (12 feet high by 4 feet wide) form, also

hardy to zone 6. 'Fiery Cascade' is the hardiest (zone 6) red-fruiting form. 'Mohave' has beautiful, heavily borne fruits that are scab resistant.

Raphiolepis indica

India-hawthorn
Zones 8B to 10
Broad-leafed evergreen

Raphiolepis is a reliable, easy-to-care-for shrub that is both beautiful and serviceable for a multitude of purposes. Its leathery, evergreen foliage and neat, dense, restrained habit, 3 to 5 feet high and wide, make it an excellent low background, mass, informal hedge, or large-scale ground cover. Use it as as a foreground or facing plant in a shrub border, or as a container plant. The flowers bloom in midwinter or spring, usually repeating in the fall, and vary from white to red, according to the cultivar. Prefers full sun but tolerates partial shade well, in addition to a variety of soils. Although reasonably tolerant of drought, it looks best when frequently watered.

Minimize splashing water onto foliage, as fireblight and leaf spots can be problems, and protect from aphids. Native to southern China.

Rhododendron species

Rhododendrons and azaleas
Hardiness varies with species
Some evergreen, some deciduous species

In addition to their beautiful flowers, rhododendrons and azaleas offer outstanding form, foliage, and many subtle qualities. Unfortunately, there are many areas in the United States where these plants do not adapt well, including the desert and the plains states, but breeding efforts are expanding this range.

Rhododendron is a complicated genus containing over nine hundred species, of which more than ten thousand named varieties are listed in the *International Register of Names*. The genus is divided into several series, one of which is azalea. Botanists are still arguing over exactly what anatomical characteristics

separate azaleas from rhododendrons. Although many azaleas are deciduous, and most rhododendrons are evergreen, both azaleas and rhododendrons have deciduous and evergreen species. Azaleas are often incorrectly thought of as being smaller in form and leaf than rhododendrons, but several rhododendrons are tiny rock-garden dwarfs with leaves smaller than any azalea. One simple distinction to remember is that, although all azaleas are rhododendrons, not all rhododendrons are azaleas.

Rhododendron, Gable hybrids (Gable hybrid azalea, zones 6 to 8)   This variable group of hybrids was bred for increased hardiness, although they should not be considered for use north of zone 6. Their evergreen foliage tends to redden and fall in the northern part of their range. The flowers appear in May, and are in the red to purple hues, with some light violets, orange-reds, and pinks.

Rhododendron × *gandavense* (Ghent hybrid azaleas, zones 5 to 8)   Many of the cultivars of this deciduous

Rhododendron canadense (rhodora)

shrub are hardy to -20° F, and some are grown as far north as zone 4 with success. Cultivars are available in a variety of colors and in single and double flowers. Usually growing 6 to 10 feet high with a comparable spread, the Ghent hybrids perform best in light shade.

Rhododendron, Indica hybrids (Indian hybrid azalea, zones 8 to 10) This group of tender, evergreen azaleas was originally developed for greenhouse forcing, but many cultivars have since been selected as landscape plants for mild climates and are common in gardens of the South and California. They are divided into two groups: Belgian and southern. The Belgian Indica hybrids are the most tender and should not be grown where temperatures fall below 15° F. The southern Indica hybrids have been selected from the Belgian hybrids for greater sun tolerance and more vigorous growth. Most are hardy to -10° F, although damage to flower buds can occur below 15° F. Flower colors for both groups range from

white through violet, pink, red, and salmon.

Rhododendron, Knapp Hill–Exbury hybrids (zones 6 to 8) Brilliant flowers cover these shrubs in late May and early June, and are available in hundreds of different colors. The flowers are large, borne in many huge trusses. The medium green deciduous foliage turns to vivid yellows, oranges, and reds in the fall. As with most deciduous azaleas, it is less particular about soil acidity and winter shade than evergreen varieties but is relatively intolerant of hot summer conditions. It generally reaches 4 to 8 feet in height with a comparable spread. Some of the newer cultivars are hardy to zone 4.

Rhododendron ×
kosteranum (Mollis hybrid azaleas, zones 5B to 7) Similar to the Ghent hybrids, these deciduous azaleas are not as hardy or long living. Cultivars are available with yellow and gold flowers through salmon and orange-red. They bloom in late May. The Mollis hybrids offered at many nurseries are actually *Rhododendron molle*

grown from seed, so select plants when in bloom. Mollis hybrid azaleas perform well in full sun and neutral soil, and grow to a restrained 3- to 8-foot rounded form.

Rhododendron × 'Loderi' (Loderi hybrid rhododendrons, zones 8 to 10) Famous for its powerful fragrance and showy flower clusters in shades of white to pink, this evergreen rhododendron should not be grown where winter temperatures fall below 0° F. Although the growth rate is slow, they become too large for most gardens, reaching an open, loose form 8 feet or more in height and width.

Rhododendron, P.J.M. hybrids (zones 5 to 8) This group of evergreen rhododendrons grows 3 to 6 feet high into a rounded, dense mass. The dark green foliage turns a deep purple in cold weather, and is sometimes deciduous in the northern extremes of its range. The flowers vary in the intensity of their bright, lavender-pink color, so buy this plant when in bloom. Flowers last into the fall in the Southeast.

Rhododendron arborescens (sweet azalea, zones 5 to 8) Producing white flowers in early June and July with a fragrance similar to heliotrope, this deciduous shrub grows 8 to 20 feet high and wide. It is cloaked with bright green leaves in the summer that turn dark red in the fall. Native from New York to Georgia and Alabama, along mountain streams and in cool mountain meadows.

Rhododendron calendulaceum (flame azalea, zones 5 to 8) The long-lasting June blooms of this deciduous eastern native range from yellow through orange and scarlet. In the fall, the fiery colors are echoed in the foliage as it changes from yellow to bronze. This shrub is variable in color, so purchase it when in bloom. Most selections reach 6 to 8 feet in height. Native from Pennsylvania through Georgia and west to Tennessee.

Rhododendron canadense (rhodora, zones 2 to 6) Found wild in bogs and in moist, very acid soils, this small, rounded, 3- to 4-foot

Rhododendron impeditum (cloudland rhododendron)

shrub has small deciduous leaves and light purple flowers in mid-May. It is most useful in a low, wet spot in a garden with cool summers. Native from Newfoundland and Labrador to New York and Pennsylvania.

Rhododendron carolinianum (Carolina rhododendron, zones 5 to 8A)   This restrained, 3- to 6-foot, rounded shrub bears white or pink flowers against dark, medium-sized, evergreen leaves. Native to the Blue Ridge Mountains of Carolina and Tennessee.

Rhododendron catawbiense (Catawba rhododendron, zones 5 to 7)   This is one of the hardiest large, evergreen rhododendrons, growing to an open 6- to 10-foot height and width in the garden, although it often reaches 15 to 20 feet in the wild. Trusses of reddish purple flowers are borne in great quantities in mid- to late May, standing out against the handsome, dark green leaves. Many cultivars are available, from bright red to purple or white, some of which are among the hardiest rhododendrons for harsh climates.

Native to the Allegheny Mountains from West Virginia to Georgia and Alabama.

Rhododendron impeditum (cloudland rhododendron, zones 5 to 8)   As with most dwarf rhododendrons, the hardiness range of this plant depends upon how well it is protected in the winter. Growing only 18 inches high and wide, with densely borne, tiny, gray-green leaves, it makes an attractive plant for a sheltered spot in a rock garden. The flowers are mauve or lavender. This shrub is more sensitive than most rhododendrons to hot, dry summers.

Rhododendron kaempferi (torch azalea, zones 6 to 8) This species and its hybrid forms are covered with flowers in May, ranging from white to rose to red-orange and salmon. The shrub can reach 5 to 6 feet high in five years, and may grow to 10 feet tall. The leaves are semi-evergreen in the north and evergreen in the south, and often turn red in cold weather. Do not plant where winter temperatures drop below -10° F. In their native Japan,

they are frequently found growing on sunny hillsides and by the sea, but their flower colors last longest with light shade. It is one of the few deciduous azaleas that flowers well in the deepest shade.

Rhododendron keiskei (Kiesk rhododendron, zones 6B to 8) This is one of the few evergreen rhododendrons to bear yellow flowers. Variable in size from a 6-inch, rock-garden shrublet to an 8-foot, open, loose shrub. All have small, finely textured leaves.

Rhododendron lapponicum (Lapland rhododendron, zones 3 to 7)   Grow this unusually hardy evergreen shrub in rock or alpine gardens where summers remain cool. Small purple flowers appear in June on a low, 1½-foot, prostrate form against tiny, dark green leaves.

Rhododendron maximum (rosebay rhododendron, zones 4 to 8)   This North American native is the tallest evergreen rhododendron hardy in the north. In the wild it can reach 30 feet, but a height of 4 to 15 feet is more likely in most northern gardens. Because the

habit is loose and open, it is best to use this plant in large masses; it can make a splendid hedge. The flowers are pink in bud and open to white or rosy purple. The flowers are borne late in the season, in June or July, but are partially hidden by the large 4- to 8-inch leaves. This rhododendron must be grown in at least partial shade to thrive.

Rhododendron mucronulatum (Korean rhododendron, zones 5 to 8) A deciduous variety, this is the first of all hardy rhododendrons and azaleas to flower in spring, with bright, rosy-purple blossoms appearing as early as mid- to late March. For this reason, it is susceptible to premature warm spells and late freezes, which can kill the flower buds overnight, so plant this shrub where it is sheltered from southern or southwestern sun in February and March. The attractive, early flowers and compact habit make it a good choice for planting near the house on the northeastern side, or in a sheltered shrub border. 'Cornell

Rhododendron periclymenoides (pinxterbloom azalea)

Rhus copallina (flameleaf sumac)

Pink' is a particularly beautiful pink form.

Rhododendron obtusum (Hiryu azaleas, zones 7 to 9) Although a few cultivars of this evergreen azalea are hardy to -10° F, many of the more tender varieties are commonly sold as far north as zone 5B, with disappointing results. In milder gardens where hardiness is not a problem, the Hiryu azalea is a reliable and popular shrub. Several of its brilliant red cultivars are especially good—'Hinodegiri', 'Hino-Crimson', and 'Hershey's Red', for example. The form is broad, low, and spreading, reaching 3 to 6 feet high and twice as wide at maturity. The small leaves give it a fine texture. The flowers appear in March and April in great quantities and range from white to pink, to lavender, to scarlet. 'Snow', 'Coral Bells', 'Pink Pearl', and 'Sherwood Red' are also fine cultivars.

Rhododendron periclymenoides (pinxterbloom azalea, zones 4 to 9) A hardy, deciduous azalea with pinkish white, fragrant flowers that bloom in late April or early May, this one features a low, neat habit, usually 4 to 6 feet wide and high. The foliage is bright green in the summer, turning to a dull yellowish brown in the fall. This shrub performs well in full sun and dry, sandy, rocky soils—a rare exception for the genus *Rhododendron.*

Rhododendron schlippenbachii (royal azalea, zones 5 to 8) The royal azalea is a deciduous, upright, rounded shrub, growing 6 to 8 feet high and wide. In the summer the foliage is a dark green; in the fall it turns a kaleidoscope of colors. The fragrant, pale pink to white flowers are borne in early to mid-May but vary in intensity among plants grown from seed, so buy this plant when it is in bloom. Unlike most other rhododendrons and azaleas, this one does not require acid soil, being comfortable with a pH range of 6.5 to 7.

Rhus copallina

Flameleaf sumac, shining sumac
Zones 5 to 8
Deciduous

Although this is the best sumac for ornamental use, few nurseries offer this plant, preferring its larger, weedier, and shorter-lived cousin, the staghorn sumac. Occasionally reaching 30 feet in the wild, this open shrub rarely exceeds 8 feet in cultivation. It spreads into clumps through suckering, but in a much more restrained and controllable manner than the staghorn sumac. Its shiny green foliage is darker than any other sumac, and the compound, large, almost tropical leaves turn a brilliant red orange in the fall. The flameleaf sumac does well in containers. It is easily transplanted and adaptable to many soils, but prefers well-drained ones and is intolerant of standing water. A long-living plant, it can be used as a specimen for fall color and interesting silhouettes. Native to easter United States.

Rhus typhina (staghorn sumac, zones 4 to 8) Although individual plants live for a short time, the profuse suckers with which this large 25-foot shrub forms massive colonies are weedy and hard to suppress. A picturesque shrub with finely textured foliage and downy stems and fruit, it has the same lovely fall color and structural interest as the flameleaf sumac. Because it dies after a few years, the staghorn sumac is not suitable as a focal specimen. It is best to reserve this shrub for massing and naturalizing in large, open areas.

Rosa species

Rose

Hardiness varies with species
Mostly deciduous, some evergreen species

The hybrid tea, floribunda, grandiflora, and climbing roses are represented by a profusion of cultivars that have placed the rose at the pinnacle of horticultural breeding. For a complete discussion of roses, consult Ortho's book *All About Roses.*

Rosa hugonis (Father Hugo rose)

Rosa rugosa (rugosa rose, saltspray rose)

Although perhaps not as well known, the species roses whose descriptions follow are of much greater use to the landscape gardener. Unlike the hobby roses mentioned above, these are generally easier to grow, pest-free, and require little special attention to pruning or feeding. Most have seasonal and short-lived (but effective) flowers, excellent foliage qualities, larger size, increased hardiness, and occasionally attractive fall fruit and foliage color.

Rosa banksiae (Lady Banks rose, zones 8 to 10)   This tender, large, semievergreen or evergreen shrub climbs on trellises and fences as high as 18 feet. Grown without support, it forms a sprawling, rambling mass 6 to 8 feet high and nearly twice as wide. The flowers are yellow fading to white and are borne in profusion. White and double-flowered forms are available. Native to China.

Rosa foetida (Austrian briar, zones 4 to 9)   The single, deep yellow flowers of this 10-foot-high-and-wide shrub

have been popular for centuries. 'Bicolor' is a form with coppery red flowers tinged with yellow. 'Persiana' has smaller, double yellow flowers. Native to western Asia.

Rosa hugonis (Father Hugo rose, zones 5 to 10)   This is one of the best and most popular of the yellow-blooming species roses. The single, canary yellow blossoms appear in May, along with the late tulips, and are thought by many to be the most exquisite rose blossom in bud. The plant grows rapidly to 6 to 8 feet high and often wider, with an upright, arching, twiggy habit. The finely cut foliage is pleasing, but this plant tends toward raggedness when not in bloom. Prune the oldest wood to the ground each year after blooming to encourage more flowering and to keep the plant neater. Use Father Hugo rose as a screen or informal hedge, in the shrub border, or espaliered on a trellis. Native to central China.

Rosa rubrifolia (redleaf rose, zones 2 to 8)   Valuable in the harsh, northern prairie states, this rose features reddish

tinged foliage. The single pink flowers in the spring are not especially attractive. Native to central Europe.

Rosa rugosa (rugosa rose, saltspray rose, zones 2 to 10)   Especially well adapted to the sandy soils and saline environment of coastal gardens, the rugosa rose is probably the easiest rose to grow. The flowers range from rose-purple to white, single or double, according to the cultivar selected. After a heavy late-spring bloom, they continue to bloom lightly all summer. Forming a dense, brambly mat 4 to 6 feet high and wide, the stout, upright, and prickly canes withstand pruning well and make an effective barrier hedge. The leaves are a deep, lustrous green that changes to yellow in the fall. They make an effective backdrop for the brick-red hips. An excellent choice for difficult, rocky or sandy soils. Native to northern China, Korea, and Japan.

Rosa spinosissima (Scotch rose, zones 4 to 10)   The free-spreading, suckering habit of this 3- to 4-foot-high shrub makes it a useful, rapidly

growing bank or ground cover, especially where erosion is a problem. It is available in a variety of flower colors, from pink to white to yellow, single or double. The blossoms are fragrant and appear in late May and early June. The low habit, profuse blooms, variety of cultivars, and ease of culture have all contributed to its popularity. Native to Europe, western Asia, and now naturalized in the northeastern United States. Despite its common name, this is the only rose native to Ireland.

Rosa virginiana (Virginia rose, zones 4 to 10)   This is another rose that is excellent by the sea, but is extremely easy to grow anywhere in well-drained soil. In addition, it is our most beautiful native rose, attractive in all seasons. The flowers are single, pink, and open in June. The foliage is a crisp, glossy dark green and unusually free from pests. In the fall it develops brilliant foliage coloration, starting with purple, then changing to orange, red, crimson, and finally yellow. The hips are bright red, borne in great

Rosa virginiana (Virginia rose)

Rosmarinus officinalis 'Collingwood Ingram' (rosemary)

quantities, and are effective into the winter. The canes add to the winter interest because of their reddish hue. This rose can grow 6 feet high and spread indefinitely by underground stems, but is easily restrained into a 3-foot hedge. Where its vigorous habit spreads too far, cut the whole shrub back to the ground; it rapidly recovers into excellent form. Native from Newfoundland to Virginia, Alabama, and Missouri.

Rosa wichuraiana (memorial rose, zones 6 to 10)   Especially in milder climates where its foliage is semievergreen or evergreen, this trailing rose makes an excellent ground cover. Spreading 8 to 16 feet or more, and achieving a maximum height of 1½ feet, it forms a dense mat of glossy, deep green foliage that few weeds can penetrate. The small, white, fragrant flowers appear in late June through July, making it one of the last rose species to bloom. Native to China, Korea, and Japan.

Rosmarinus officinalis

Rosemary
Zones 7b to 8
Narrow-leafed evergreen

Best in mild, Mediterranean climates with dry summers and wet winters, this is the rosemary familiar to cooks. Its evergreen, fragrant foliage clips and shears well. Use larger types as a clipped hedge or in the dry shrub border. Lower types make excellent erosion-controlling bank or ground covers, spilling over rocks and walls. Size varies according to variety, from 2 to 6 feet high and often twice as wide. The showy flowers are light blue and appear in late winter or very early spring. Certain cultivars such as 'Collingwood Ingram', 'Lockwood de Forest', and 'Tuscan Blue' have been selected for bright blue flowers. The shrub is attractive to birds and bees. Rosemary must have sharp drainage; overwatering and overfertilizing results in rank, stretchy growth. It tolerates heat, sun, infertile soil, and drought. Set

ground cover varieties 2 feet apart for a quick cover. Native to southern Europe and Asia Minor.

Spiraea species

Spirea
Zones 5 to 10
Deciduous

The most familiar spireas are bridal wreath or Vanhoutte spirea, two traditional favorites that are as awkward, large, and cumbersome as they are popular. Although many superior, more dwarfed varieties are available, no spirea is particularly attractive when not in bloom. Easily transplanted, fast growing, and low in maintenance, spireas are not particular about soil. Although they are subject to many pests, including fireblight, leaf spot, powdery mildew, and a host of insects, none appears to be fatally serious if the plant is placed in a location with full sun and good air circulation. Spireas differ as to when they should be pruned. Summer-flowering types should be pruned in late winter or early spring as they

bloom on the current year's wood; spring-flowering types should be pruned directly after blooming. Older, leggy plants of either type can be renewed by cutting them to the ground in early spring. Use spireas in a shrub border as an inexpensive, fast-growing, and easy-to-care-for filler, where their dull nonblooming appearance can be masked. The lower-growing types make passable coarse ground covers.

Spiraea × bumalda (bumalda spirea)   This low, spreading shrub grows 2 to 3 feet high and 3 to 5 feet wide, with white to deep pink flowers blooming from mid-June to August on the current year's growth. Native to Japan. 'Anthony Waterer' is a popular deep rose cultivar, but several other superior cultivars are available. They include 'Crispa' (growing 2 feet high with twisted leaves), 'Gold Flame' (low growing with brightly colored red, copper, and orange foliage in early spring and fall), and 'Nyeswood' (especially dense and compact with pink flowers).

Spiraea × *bumalda* 'Anthony Waterer' (bumalda spirea)

Syringa vulgaris (common lilac)

Spiraea × *vanhouttei* (Vanhoutte spirea)   A fast-growing spirea, it becomes an 8- to 10-foot-high, arching, fountainlike shrub, spreading 10 to 12 feet. This tough shrub is used in the border and for massing. Its size definitely limits it to large gardens. The white flowers are effective from early April to May and appear on old wood.

Spiraea albiflora (Japanese white spirea)   This low (1½ feet), rounded, dense shrub has white flowers that produce on the current year's growth in late June and July. The neat, compact habit makes it superior to many other spireas. Native to Japan.

Spiraea japonica (Japanese spirea)   This is similar to *S.* × *bumalda*, except for a larger, coarser habit that grows 4 to 5 feet high. 'Atrosanguinea' is a superior, deep rose-red cultivar that grows from 2½ to 4 feet high and is hardier (zone 4B). The Japanese spirea blooms on new wood from early June through July. Native to Japan.

Spirea nipponica tosaensis 'Snowmound' (snowmound spirea)   A dwarfish, white-blooming spirea that grows 3 to 5 feet high and as wide, it is superior to the Vanhoutte spirea because of its denser, neater, more compact form. Native to Japan.

Spiraea prunifolia (bridal-wreath spirea)   This species is a rangy, coarse, open shrub, growing 4 to 9 feet tall and 6 to 8 feet wide. The dull white flowers appear in April on old wood. Native to Korea, China, and Taiwan.

Symplocos paniculata

Sapphireberry, Asiatic sweetleaf
Zones 5 to 8
Deciduous

Brilliant, unusual blue fruits—often described as turquoise or azure—practically cover this shrub in the fall. These are the truest blue of any so-called blue-fruited shrubs available, and are a real eye-catcher in the garden. Unfortunately, they are frequently as attrac-tive to birds as they are to people. The profuse, creamy white powderpuff flowers that bloom in May and June are more showy than many other favorites such as deutzia, honeysuckle, and mockorange. Sapphireberry grows to 10 to 20 feet tall and wide, and fruit production varies from plant to plant. For more dependable fruit production, plant two or more together for cross fertilization. Transplants easily into any well-drained soil. Full sun is best for optimum fruit production. Long living and pest-free, it is a dependable bloomer whose flower buds are hardy to -25° F. This shrub is seldom offered by nurseries. Native to rocky slopes, edges of woods, and forest glades in full sun from the Himalayas to Japan.

Syringa vulgaris

Common lilac
Zones 3B to 7 (somewhat successful farther south)
Deciduous

The common lilac is a wonderful plant for the rear of a shrub border or any out-of-the-way place where its scent can be appreciated. However, because it is only attractive and fragrant during its few weeks in bloom, it is not useful as a specimen or in highly visible spots. A large, upright, often irregular shrub growing 20 feet in height and 12 to 15 feet in spread, the leaves are gray to dark green or bluish green, and are often covered with powdery mildew by mid-summer. A great profusion of cultivars is available for flower color.

Although common lilacs live a long time and survive most conditions, they are not easy to keep looking attractive. They normally produce good flowers only every other year. Plant in full sun in neutral, rich soil high in organic matter. Although they respond well to light and annual fertilization, too much decreases flowering. Remove spent blossoms immediately to increase next year's bloom, and prune out 50 to 75 percent of the basal suckers each year. Renew old plants by cutting them back almost to the ground. Lilacs are plagued by many diseases and insects.

Tamarix hispida 'Summer Cloud' (Kashgar tamarisk)

Taxus species (yew)

Most lilacs do not perform well in mild climates. Exceptions are cultivars selected for this purpose, including 'Lavender Lady', 'Blue Boy', Chiffon', 'Mrs. Forrest K. Smith', and 'Sylvan Beauty'. Native to southern Europe.

Tamarix hispida

Kashgar tamarisk
Zones 5 to 10
Deciduous

For a bright pink August to September display under the harshest seashore conditions, try this slender, wispy, 4- to 6-foot shrub. Like every tamarisk, it is unattractive in winter and should be hidden in the shrub border. It is the most restrained of the tamarisks for the small garden. The foliage is needlelike, similar to junipers, but deciduous, creating a feathery, light-green effect. Tamarisk must have well-drained soil and is touchy about transplanting, so purchase young, container-grown plants. It is tolerant of salty, sandy soil, harsh, dry winds, and drought. Although it makes an excellent choice

for desert gardens, it will need periodic watering. If the soil is too fertile, it becomes leggy and rangy. All tamarisk plants grow rapidly. Prune when dormant in early spring. Native to the region of the Caspian Sea.

Tamarix parviflora (smallflowered tamarisk, zones 5 to 10)   Similar in form and flower to *T. ramosissima*, this one flowers on old wood, so prune it hard each year just after flowering. Native to southeastern Europe.

Tamarix ramosissima, also called *T. pentandra* and *T. chinensis* (five-stamen tamarisk, zones 2 to 10)   This is the hardiest tamarisk and is larger, leggier, and more awkward than *T. hispida*, growing 10 to 15 feet high, 20 to 30 feet in mild climates. Because it flowers on new growth, cut back hard or even to the ground after the leaves drop in the fall. Its root system can become invasive. It performs well in coastal gardens and the arid Southwest. In mild areas it readily naturalizes, often becoming difficult to handle. Native from southeastern Europe to central Asia.

Taxus species

Yew
Zones 5 and 6B to 8
Conifer

Although the yew species include large, 40- to 50-foot-high trees, the many cultivars available are among the most useful coniferous evergreen shrubs for the landscape. Hardy and trouble-free, with dark green foliage and a variety of dense, refined forms, yews are often planted without consideration for their ultimate size, so select the appropriate variety. Yews accept formal pruning well and are often clipped into hedges or other shapes. Consider them also for massing, as an evergreen touch to the shrub border, and as a foundation plant. When allowed to develop their natural forms, the effect is usually graceful and appealing. Given soil with excellent drainage, yews prove to be generally easy to grow and pest-free, in sun or shade. In heavy, wet soils they are stunted and sickly, if they survive at all. Give them adequate moisture and protect

them from sweeping wind. In hot, dry climates, give them a northern exposure and hose the foliage frequently during the driest periods. Beware of their colorful, red fruits, the inner portions of which are poisonous.

Taxus × *media* (Anglojap yew, zones 5 to 10)   A hybrid between the following two species, this yew has a wide variety of cultivars from low, spreading types to tall, narrow ones.

Taxus baccata (English yew, zones 6B to 10)   This least hardy yew has several cultivars that are excellent for southern gardens. Native throughout Europe.

Taxus cuspidata (Japanese yew, Zones 5 to 10)   Many excellent cultivars of this species are available, ranging from 'Aurescens', a low, 1-foot-high and 3-feet-wide form with yellow new growth, to 'Capitata', a 40- to 50-foot pyramidal form. Native to Japan and Korea.

Thuja occidentalis 'Globosa' (American arborvitae)

Tsuga canadensis 'Pendula' (Sargent's weeping hemlock)

Vaccinium corymbosum (highbush blueberry)

Thuja occidentalis

American arborvitae
Zones 2 to 10
Conifer

This is actually a large, up-right, coniferous tree growing 40 to 60 feet tall, but many slow-growing cultivars have been selected that are often used in foundation plantings, as hedges, or as screens. Varieties range from inches-high, rock-garden plants to 20-foot, columnar small trees that are useful as screens. Most cultivars turn yellow-brown in cold weather, although 'Nigra' and 'Techny' retain dark green foliage all winter long. Plant arborvitae in well-drained moist soil in full sun. It is tolerant of highly alkaline soils and performs best in areas of high atmospheric moisture. The branches and foliage are quite susceptible to damage from winter winds, snow, and ice. Although many pests are listed as potential problems, these plants are generally easy to care for and trouble-free. Native from Nova Scotia and Manitoba south to the Carolinas and Tennessee.

Tsuga canadensis 'Pendula'

Sargent's weeping hemlock
Zones 4 to 8B
Conifer

This, the most commonly grown dwarf hemlock, displays a graceful, pendulous habit and refined evergreen foliage. Although it can reach 5 to 6 feet in height and two or three times that in spread in extreme old age, a more reasonable size to expect in one lifetime is 3 to 4 feet high by 8 to 9 feet wide. This plant makes an outstanding focal specimen. Plant it in well-drained, moist, acid soil. Unlike most conifers it prefers partial shade. If drainage is good, the soil is moist, and if there are no drying winds it tolerates full sun. Hemlock does not tolerate wind, drought, or waterlogged soils, and in areas where summer temperatures exceed 95° F, it is likely to develop leaf scorch. This is not a plant for heavily polluted areas. If the location is right, hemlock is usually a trouble-free and long-living plant. Native from

Nova Scotia to Minnesota, and south along the mountains to Alabama and Georgia.

Vaccinium corymbosum

Highbush blueberry
Zones 4 to 8A
Deciduous

Primarily grown for its delicious fruit, the highbush blueberry makes an outstanding ornamental plant when given the right growing conditions. It is a fairly large shrub, often reaching 6 to 12 feet high and 8 to 12 feet wide, but grows slowly and is easily restrained. Its dark, almost blue-green, lustrous foliage consistently turns into bright yellow, bronze, orange, or red combinations in the fall, and densely covers a rounded, compact form. Just as the leaves emerge in May, small white flowers are borne in great quantities, followed by the fruits that ripen in late July through August.

If given moist, acid (pH 4.5 to 5.5), well-drained soil that is high in organic matter, blueberries are generally an easy

plant to grow. They perform best in sandy, acid soils. Mulch well to promote a cool, moist root run, give them full sun to partial shade, and regular, adequate moisture. When blueberries are grown commercially for fruit, regular spraying and protection from birds is necessary. Grown in the landscape for ornamental purposes, their fruit yield is generally sufficient without any elaborate precautions. Use highbush blueberries as a tasty and attractive addition to a shrub border, in a foundation planting, or massed naturally in large areas. Native from Maine to Minnesota and south to Florida and Louisiana.

Viburnum species

Hardiness varies with species
Some evergreen, some deciduous species

Viburnum is a diverse genus that contains a wide range of valuable shrubs for the garden. Some are grown for their moderately attractive and powerfully fragrant blossoms;

Viburnum dilatatum 'Iroquois' (linden viburnum)

Viburnum opulus (European cranberrybush)

others display showy combinations of flower, fruit, and fall color. Most perform best in a moist, well-drained soil that is slightly acid, although they are generally quite adaptable to other soils. Many insects and diseases can attack viburnums, although these shrubs are usually untroubled if kept vigorous.

Viburnum × burkwoodii (Burkwood viburnum, zones 6 to 10) This is an upright, somewhat straggly shrub, 8 to 10 feet high and 5 to 7 feet wide, grown primarily for its fragrant blossoms that are pink opening to white and appear in early to late April before the leaves appear. It is a fine plant for a shrub border, where its fragrance can perfume an entire garden. In southern gardens the foliage is evergreen.

Viburnum × carlcephalum (fragrant snowball viburnum, zones 6 to 9) This is another delightfully fragrant shrub that produces white flowers in late April or May. Its loose, open growth, 6 to 10 feet high and wide, blends well into the shrub border.

Viburnum × juddii (Judd viburnum, zones 5 to 10) The Judd viburnum is similar to *Viburnum carlesii*, except that it is more reliably hardy in northern zone 5.

Viburnum × rhytidophylloides (lantanaphyllum viburnum, zones 6 to 10) Best known for the cultivar 'Willowwood', this is a large shrub, 8 to 10 feet tall and wide, with large, coarse, leathery leaves that remain a dark green throughout the winter. It is slightly hardier than its parent, *V. rhytidophyllum*, performing well under harsh midwestern prairie conditions. The coarse texture of the foliage is accentuated in the winter when the leaves hang limply on the stems. Flowers and fruits are largely uninteresting.

Viburnum carlesii (Koreanspice viburnum, zones 5 to 8) A popular fragrance shrub for northern gardens, this viburnum produces pinkish-white flowers in late April to early May that have a spicy, sweet scent. It grows rounded, dense, 4 to 5 feet high and 4 to 8

feet wide, occasionally reaching a height of 8 feet. Native to Korea.

Viburnum davidii (David viburnum, zones 8 to 10) This small (1 to 3 feet high and 3 to 4 feet wide), dense, large-leafed, evergreen shrub does well in southern gardens. The dark, metallic blue fruits on this shrub are especially appealing. Native to China.

Viburnum dilatatum (linden viburnum, zones 5B to 8) This upright, open shrub grows 8 to 10 feet high and 5 to 8 feet wide. The white flowers in May and June are a welcome attraction, but the most outstanding season is in September and October when the fruits ripen. The bright red fruits often remain effective into December. Most effectively used in a shrub border, where its tendency to become leggy can be minimized. Plant several together, as cross fertilization improves fruiting. Native to eastern Asia.

Viburnum macrocephalum (Chinese snowball viburnum, zones 7 to 10) Its white, round balls of sterile flowers

borne in late May to early June are the largest flower clusters of any viburnum, often 8 inches in diameter. In the northern part of its range it needs protection from winter winds, and it must have well-drained soil. It is a dense, rounded shrub, 6 to 10 feet high and wide, and in southern areas it is semievergreen.

Viburnum opulus (European cranberrybush, zones 4 to 10) This is an effective shrub because of its delicate white, pinwheel flowers in mid-May. The sterile showy flowers are on the outside of the cluster, while the fertile, less conspicuous flowers are on the inside of the cluster. Bright red, berrylike fruits are effective from September to November, and are accompanied by fall foliage color. This is a large shrub, growing 8 to 12 feet high (possibly 15 feet), and spreading 10 to 15 feet. Use in large gardens in a border, as a screen, or for massing. It is susceptible to aphids (especially 'Rosea'), which disfigure young leaves. For this reason, *Viburnum trilobum*, a nearly identical

Viburnum plicatum var. *tomentosum* (doublefile viburnum)

Xylosma congestum (shiny xylosma)

American native, is recommended as a substitute. 'Compactum' is a dense, dwarf variety that is about half the size of the species. 'Nanum' is another dwarf that bears no flowers or fruits.

Viburnum plicatum var. *tomentosum* (doublefile viburnum, zones 5 to 9)   Many experts consider this the most beautiful of all flowering deciduous shrubs. The profuse but lacy, pure white pinwheel-flowers that bloom in May are gracefully arranged along the horizontally tiered, stratified branches. In the summer the foliage is dark green, and in the fall it displays autumn color. The bright red fruits ripen in July and August and are attractive to birds. Growing 8 to 10 feet high and slightly wider, this shrub makes an excellent focal specimen, and is a perfect horizontal complement to the upright-oriented shrub border. It combines well with broad-leafed evergreens, and is effective against dark red brick backgrounds or with red-blooming flowers, such as some azaleas. Foundation plantings, masses, and screens are also good uses for this shrub. Doublefile viburnum does not tolerate heavy, wet soils. Planted in fertile, well-drained but moist soil, it is generally an easily maintained, trouble-free plant. Native to China and Japan. Many superior cultivars have been selected for their form, flowers, and fruits, such as 'Mariesii' (largest flowers and best fruits) and 'Pink Beauty' (smaller flowers and leaves with outstanding deep pink blooms).

Viburnum tinus (laurustinus, zones 8 to 10)   An evergreen, 6- to 12-foot-high, upright shrub grown in southern and western gardens for its dark green foliage, pink-turning-to-white flowers and bright, metallic blue fruit. Its dense foliage hugs the ground, making it excellent for screens and hedges. It responds well to formal pruning. Well adapted to shade, it flowers more profusely in full sun. Native to the Mediterranean region of Europe.

Viburnum trilobum (American cranberrybush viburnum, zones 3 to 9)   This shrub is similar in all respects to *Viburnum opulus*, and being hardier and much more resistant to aphids, it makes an excellent substitute. 'Compactum' is a fine dwarf form that produces excellent flowers and fruits. Unlike those of *V. opulus*, the fruits of *V. trilobum* make tasty jams and jellies. Native to New Brunswick to British Columbia, south to New York and Oregon.

Weigela florida

Old-fashioned weigela
Zones 5 to 8
Deciduous

Out of bloom, the old-fashioned weigela is a coarse, usually rangy shrub that requires considerable pruning to keep it presentable. In bloom it is spectacular. In late May to early June it is laden with rosy pink blooms. Use weigela in the shrub border, in masses, and in groupings, where its form and texture can be hidden when not in bloom. Many cultivars and hybrids are available, from white to deep red flowers. It prefers well-drained soil and a sunny location, but weigela is nevertheless quite adaptable and pest-free. Prune after flowering to clean up the shrub's appearance. The variety *venusta* is the hardiest weigela (zone 4), with finely textured leaves and rosy pink flowers. Native to northern China and Korea.

Xylosma congestum

Shiny xylosma
Zones 8 to 10
Broad-leafed evergreen

Valued for its yellow-green foliage in all seasons, shiny xylosma grows slowly to be a rounded, loose shrub or small tree 8 to 10 feet high and wide. Some forms are spiny and make useful barriers. Also use xylosma in a shrub border or foundation planting, as a container plant, as a formal or informal hedge, or for a high bank or ground cover. Plant it in any soil. It tolerates heat and drought but looks best when it has adequate water. Native to southern China.

Climate Zone Map

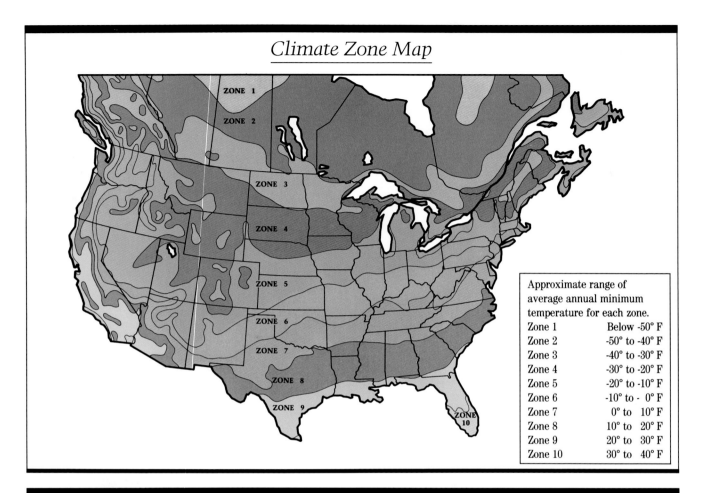

Approximate range of average annual minimum temperature for each zone.	
Zone 1	Below -50° F
Zone 2	-50° to -40° F
Zone 3	-40° to -30° F
Zone 4	-30° to -20° F
Zone 5	-20° to -10° F
Zone 6	-10° to - 0° F
Zone 7	0° to 10° F
Zone 8	10° to 20° F
Zone 9	20° to 30° F
Zone 10	30° to 40° F

U.S. Measure and Metric Measure Conversion Chart

		Formulas for Exact Measures			Rounded Measures for Quick Reference		
	Symbol	When you know:	Multiply by:	To find:			
Mass	oz	ounces	28.35	grams	1 oz		= 30 g
(Weight)	lb	pounds	0.45	kilograms	4 oz		= 115 g
	g	grams	0.035	ounces	8 oz		= 225 g
	kg	kilograms	2.2	pounds	16 oz	= 1 lb	= 450 g
					32 oz	= 2 lb	= 900 g
					36 oz	= 2¼ lb	= 1000g (1 kg)
Volume	pt	pints	0.47	liters	1 c	= 8 oz	= 250 ml
	qt	quarts	0.95	liters	2 c (1 pt)	= 16 oz	= 500 ml
	gal	gallons	3.785	liters	4 c (1 qt)	= 32 oz	= 1 liter
	ml	milliliters	0.034	fluid ounces	4 qt (1 gal)	= 128 oz	= 3¾ liter
Length	in.	inches	2.54	centimeters	⅜ in.	= 1 cm	
	ft	feet	30.48	centimeters	1 in.	= 2.5 cm	
	yd	yards	0.9144	meters	2 in.	= 5 cm	
	mi	miles	1.609	kilometers	2½ in.	= 6.5 cm	
	km	kilometers	0.621	miles	12 in. (1 ft)	= 30 cm	
	m	meters	1.094	yards	1 yd	= 90 cm	
	cm	centimeters	0.39	inches	100 ft	= 30 m	
					1 mi	= 1.6 km	
Temperature	°F	Fahrenheit	⅝ (after subtracting 32)	Celsius	32°F	= 0°C	
	°C	Celsius	⅝ (then add 32)	Fahrenheit	212°F	= 100°C	
Area	in.²	square inches	6.452	square centimeters	1 in.²	= 6.5 cm²	
	ft²	square feet	929.0	square centimeters	1 ft²	= 930 cm²	
	yd²	square yards	8361.0	square centimeters	1 yd²	= 8360 cm²	
	a.	acres	0.4047	hectares	1 a.	= 4050 m²	